called to die

11-11-21

called to die

The story of American linguist
Chet Bitterman, a martyr for
Bible translation.

STEVE ESTES

For current information on the persecuted Church,
Please Contact:

The Voice of the Martyrs, Inc.
P.O. Box 443
Bartlesville, OK 74005
(918)337-8015

Wycliffe®

Partners in Bible Translation

Copyright © 1986 Copyright assigned to
Wycliffe Bible Translators

Library of Congress Cataloging in Publications Data
Estes, Steve.
Called to Die.

1. Bitterman, Chester Allen 1952–1981.
2. Christian biography—United States.
3. Christian biography—Columbia.
4. Persecution—Columbia. I. Title.
BR1725.B572E87 1986 266'.0092 1 [B] 85-26529
ISBN 0-938978-40-3

Edited by John D. Sloan
Line drawings by Lorin Zechiel

Printed in the United States of America

Reprinted in 2008

Because of my father, Charles Estes, I am a rich man. He loves God and serves people more than anyone I know. He has laid down his life for my sister and me and our families, and has kindled within me a passion for God and a love for books (only, he sometimes bends the pages down). I love you, Dad.

Because of my mother, Frances Estes, I feel loved. No one is more thoughtful and self-sacrificing. I have always felt free to bring friends to her home—a pleasant place to be, full of good sights and smells, that reflect her warmth and organization. She is intelligent and fun to be with. I love it when she laughs. I love you, Mom.

CONTENTS

ACKNOWLEDGMENTS

Several technical matters regarding translation work and the organization of Wycliffe Bible Translators/The Summer Institute of Linguistics have been simplified for a general audience. Out of respect for their privacy, the names and nationalities of some people have been changed.

Proper names in Spanish have been Anglicized by the removal of accent marks. In quoted Spanish conversation, the accents remain.

The conversation of Mary Bitterman with Radio Toledar in chapter 15 and the guerrilla news conferences in chapter 17 are taken directly from tapes or tape transcripts, with minimal editing.

Many people involved in Chet's life have checked this account for accuracy. In places where their recollections conflicted, I employed the following principles: (1) omission of most materials of which I was not positive; (2) attachment of special weight to the majority opinion of eyewitnesses; (3) assignment of greater value to people's accounts of their own actions than to others' statements about the same; (4) reliance primarily on diary-newspaper dating rather than upon memory or later reconstruction.

I am grieved not to be able to thank publicly, by name, each of the two hundred or so people that assisted me in this writing project. Your names and faces are in my heart. Of extraordinary value are the contributions of Lee and Lynn Henriksen, who hosted us in Colombia at their own expense; Phil Horning, my Elverson editor (this man of considerable literary talents placed himself at my disposal unstintingly for several years; I love him for it); Verna (you are such a good wife!); Bob Whitesides (whose incredible memory enhanced this book and whose friendship enhanced my life).

I am indebted to Al Wheeler, Jim Walton, Joel Stolte, Kathy Williams, Cecil Hawkins, Will Kindberg, and others of SIL in Colombia who went out of their way to be helpful. Lorin Zechiel produced fine sketches despite the difficulties of overseas communication by mail. Helen Tielmann translated many Spanish newspaper articles and transcripts for me. Jon Clemmer, Karen Brown, Laurie Thompson, Melissa Horning and Daryl Platt read the entire manuscript and offered suggestions (perhaps they will buy a copy of the book since they are mentioned here). The Stoltzfuses graciously gave me office space in their home. A number of people at Columbia Bible College helped me, including alumni. I put miles of wear on Joni Tada's and Joel McCall's computers. John Sloan, my Zondervan editor, worked late nights and became my friend as well.

Brenda shared so openly with me, and her father George Gardner did a thousand and one things for me. The Bittermans made me feel like family (Curt, thanks for all those encouraging phone calls). Bernie May's patience and kind words kept me from drowning. My friends at Community Evangelical Church, Elverson, Pennsylvania, and many people elsewhere prayed for me when I thought I would never finish.

Costa Rica, September 13, 1978. The situation in Nicaragua is getting worse. If Nicaragua falls, I guess the rest of Central America will, too. Maybe this is just some kind of self-inflicted martyr complex, but I find this recurring thought that perhaps God will call me to be martyred for Him in His service in Colombia. I am willing.

(From the diary of Chet Bitterman, eight months before he entered Colombia.)

Callers

January 19, 1981, Bogota, Colombia

In an upstairs bedroom, shortly before dawn, a young American mother sat on the edge of a steel-framed bed, rocking her nursing daughter. Beside them lay the baby's sister, half lost under the blanket that draped from the top bunk. The tiles had begun to chill the woman's feet, but her slippers were out of reach and she was too comfortable to rouse herself for them. Besides, she did not want to break the stillness. Stillness was hard to come by these days with children, and planning, and packing, and going. Always going.

Through a stifled yawn she glanced to the other end of the room where her husband dozed, face down, hugging the pillow like a little boy. It was good to see him sleep; he was worn out, too. She studied the contrast of tan shoulders against the sheets.

From downstairs the doorbell shot its startling tone through the halls. As the echo faded her eyes shifted about, then settled in front of her, focusing on nothing in particular. Odd, she thought; but Hank would take care of it.

* * *

Hank Thimell, his hair a tousled mass, stood and glared through the peephole, wondering who on earth had the nerve to come calling before breakfast. The tiny lens distorted the figure on the porch. How did anyone expect to be recognized at this time of morning? But his eyes adjusted and he could make out the figure of a policeman. "Gotta be kidding," he mumbled. He mustered as pleasant a look as he could, then unbolted the door and stepped back, prepared to be polite.

The caller entered and smoothly leveled a pistol at Hank's chest. Six armed comrades appeared from nowhere and the door clicked shut.

The pounding on her bedroom door seemed to the young mother like a bad dream. "Honey, don't open it," she wanted to say, but the words froze in her throat.

He reached for the knob and peeked out. The door exploded open.

"Vístanse! Vístanse!" A hooded man, his automatic weapon poised, filled the doorway. For a moment the young couple remained motionless.

"Vístanse!" the man barked.

"Do what?" Brenda asked.

"Get dressed," said Chet.

Slowly, Brenda fished a pair of slacks from the stack of folded laundry on the opposite bed and began an embarrassed attempt to exchange her flannel gown for street clothes. Her eyes alternated between Chet, pulling on his brown corduroys, and the gunman. A ski cap covered much of the man's face; all she could see was his bushy mustache.

"Rápido," he urged as their eyes met.

But she would not be hurried. Fighting for calmness she slipped on her watch—if they were taken somewhere to a windowless cell, she would still know day from night. She thought of Esther's blanket. It would be chilly outside. They would need shoes. She would not be rushed out barefooted just to save these gangsters a few seconds. She got her loafers under the bed. A final glance around: Had she left anything? She wrapped the baby and stood to leave. It was then that she noticed the trembling in her knees. Grabbing a book off the nightstand, she walked out of the room.

Chet followed. The guard pivoted with him as he made his way, unruffled, to the hall closet for a shirt. "I've got another daughter in there," Chet said in easy Spanish and motioned back toward the bedroom. Permission granted. Brenda started down the steps alone with the baby, her thoughts simmering.

Who are they? What are they . . . ? As she stared at her feet the sight of a police uniform crossed her line of vision on the steps below. A uniform? Something was out of place. Then she realized. The law had arrived.

She gave a murmur of relief and her face relaxed. The policeman was escorting her safely toward the first floor, his comforting arm around her shoulder. The logistics of their rescue did not concern her; others would handle that. Chet would join her in a moment.

Somewhere upstairs a cannon roared.

Her body stiffened. Strangely, the officer seemed not to notice, his only reaction a tightened grip around her shoulder.

"Todo esta bien, Señorá." He sounded too nice, like a funeral home attendant.

What do you mean, Everything is all right? Brenda's thoughts scrambled, hot. How do you know? My husband and daughter are up there. Who are you to say everything's all right?

Yes, who are you? The answer came to her as she entered the living room. There her fellow residents were herded together on the floor at gun point. Suddenly the arm around her became loathsome. She repulsed it and seated herself on the sofa against the wall.

Within minutes all sixteen occupants of the home had been rounded up into the living room: five men, five children, and six women. Some still wore robes and bed clothes. The children sat wide-eyed on the sofas, cuddled by their mothers. Everyone else lay on the floor, their wrists bound behind them to their feet.

The colorful Indian wall hangings seemed out of place, as did the fireplace, upright piano, and coffee table dotted with back issues of *National Geographic* and *Readers Digest*. No one wept, but fear showed on several faces. Others showed a calm alertness.

Chet was one of these. To Brenda's relief he had descended the stairs shortly after the gunshot, three-year-old Anna in his arms. A gunman had accidentally discharged his pistol into the wall. That was all. But Chet was without his contact lenses and stumbled toward the guard below him. His clumsiness earned him shoves and threats. "Don't speak any Spanish," he whispered as he joined his friends on the floor. He paid for the comment with a kick to the ribs.

"Mommy, why is my daddy tied up?"

A three-year-old boy perched with his blanket between brother and sister on the couch, wanted to know.

"We're playing a game."

"Why do those men have guns?"

"It's a game."

"Are they gonna shoot them?"

His mother stared up at the gunmen.

"No, Nicholas." Her gaze did not waver. "They won't shoot them."

Brenda held baby Esther close and studied the terrorists patrolling the room. Most wore casual clothes. One had a suit and tie and one a ski mask, although the sweat soon drove him to remove it. All of them wore gloves. The squeak of their shoe leather was the only sound. The men were gentlemen, for the most part. In the bedrooms several had turned their heads as the ladies dressed. Still, one sneering man waved his machine gun in everyone's face. The leaders seemed to be a policeman and a stone-faced woman in her early twenties. She wore light brown jeans with a beige sweater and looked very much at home with her automatic weapon.

The guerrillas broke. One strode toward the back office to rummage through desk drawers. Another was dispatched upstairs to search the bedrooms.

The rest remained and got down to business. Unskilled in English, the interrogators insisted on Spanish only. Señor Al Wheeler—Where is he? Silence. Do you know where he is? No, we don't. Can you give us his number? No, we can't.

Thrust of a gun barrel.

You, tell us where he is. I'm new here; I don't know. You, is he new here? Yes, he is. What's your name? Fred Gross. What do you do? Mechanic. What's his name? Fred Gross. What does he do? He's a mechanic.

Disgust.

Where's Wheeler? I'm not sure. Why not? Don't live here. Does he live here? No. Who are you? Beth Newell. What do you do? I work in literacy. What does she do? She works in literacy. Take us to Al Wheeler. I can't. Why not? Don't know where he lives.

You, where does he live? I'm not sure. What is your name? Chester Bitterman. What do you do? I'm a linguist (excellent accent). What does he do? He's a linguist.

This last information drew a response. They ignored the others momentarily—many of whom needed no theatrics to speak poor Spanish—and focused on the man whose inflections interested them as much as his occupation. A few more questions. Some promising answers. They paused to consider. This could be the one.

"You fellows get a chance to sign the guest book?"

Chet grinned. For a second everyone relaxed. (Brenda did not. Why couldn't her husband keep his own advice?) Then the break was over. Someone was sent for car keys. Electrician Pete Manier and Helena, the Colombian maid, were taken into a side office. Pete would disconnect the phones and radio; Helena would supply information.

For Pete, the sunshine that peeked through the ceiling window was out of character. It should be raining, he thought, even hailing. He and his family had arrived from the States only four days ago. If they got out of this alive, they would catch the first flight home.

They reached the end of the room where a desk, phone, radio, and telex machine made up an office.

"Desconéctelo," the ski-capped guard ordered Pete.

Pete sat on the swivel chair and began to dismount the devices. Helena stood alongside, squeezing the life from a tissue. Pete had wrapped the wires and was standing to leave when he noticed Helena's eyes fixed in front of her. He saw why. An arm's length away, taped to the wall, was a typed page.

COLOMBIAN BRANCH:
SUMMER INSTITUTE OF LINGUISTICS
PERSONNEL, UNLISTED NUMBERS,
ADDRESSES

His captors must be blind.

"Levántelo."

He lifted the radio from the table and started with his guard for the kitchen. One guerrilla remained with Helena. Pete had one foot on the stair up to the kitchen when he heard the woman lunge. He whirled about.

She had ripped the paper from the wall and was crumpling it in her hand. Her guard grabbed her wrist. She shrieked and clawed, determined to destroy it. The man stopped. He cocked his pistol an inch from her head. The paper was his. A gun poked Pete on and he could hear Helena weeping behind him.

The next hour passed quickly. Pete lugged radio equipment through the house to the Ford station wagon in the rear garage. Rejoining the others he sat with his back to the wall, pretending to be tied. Once, the doorbell rang. The guerrillas froze, signaled one another, and forced Pete's wife to open the door ("Slowly, Señora"). A minute later the caller—another maid—was bound to a chair.

Chet and another man were forced into the guerrilla van parked out front. There was discussion. Hesitation. They were brought back in. The other man was retied; Chet was steered to the rear office. On the way he passed the living room where Brenda and the policeman were talking.

"You understand, of course, it's a matter of national sovereignty. Nothing personal."

The policeman paused, assuring himself she had understood. Her Spanish was only passable.

"We tried to get you. out before, but you wouldn't listen. Now it comes to this."

Brenda mulled the statement over.

"And if this doesn't work?" Her voice was soft.

"Violence."

"You know who you're really fighting against, don't you?"

"Sure." His tone belied his answer.

From his position on the floor, mechanic Fred Gross followed their conversation pessimistically. He had first believed the guerrillas would barricade themselves inside the house; just last year an urban terrorist group had held fourteen ambassadors and a host of others hostage for over two months at the Dominican Republic Embassy downtown. This could be the same group. But here in the guest house there were children. Who would sponsor a stage-in with five whining toddlers? Bad publicity. A drain on the nerves.

Maybe they would cart everyone away. . . . But then, a sixteen-person abduction? Too much could go wrong. They probably wanted to leave. Yet they were taking their time to getting what they wanted. They had asked for Wheeler, but since he wasn't in . . . . The thought revolted and scared him, but Fred was fairly certain what would soon happen. He wondered if Brenda knew.

All this time, conversation and an occasional chuckle could be heard from the back room where Chet sat, unbound, conversing with his captors.

"I can take you to Señor Wheeler's house, but to tell you the truth, he's not your man."

"Meaning what?"

"Meaning he's not the branch director." Chet's uncombed hair and crossed legs made him look almost relaxed. "The director's at Lomalinda."

"That's okay. We don't need Wheeler anyway."

"Meaning what?" Chet asked.

"Meaning we have you." The answer was no surprise.

"I can't take you anywhere without my contacts."

"Your what?"

"Contacts. Glasses. I can't see to drive or anything without them."

"Where are they?"

"In my room."

"Get them."

Chet and his guard climbed upstairs and got the lenses. The guerrillas clustered about the open bathroom door to watch the foreigner put in his contacts.

It was time to go. The children were squirming on the couch and the gunmen were anxious to leave. One kept watch by the curtains. Guerrillas throughout the building returned to discuss the final arrangement.

Chet stood, compliant but uncringing, between his guards. The policeman raised a pistol to Chet's neck and issued instructions.

"Please," asked Brenda, "let Chet repeat it in English so we're sure to understand."

The commander nodded. Chet turned toward his family and friends. Slowly he spoke the first English that had been voiced in over an hour.

"He says you're to stay put for three hours. Don't even move. He says absolutely under no condition are you to respond to anyone from outside before that time. He says if you do they'll kill me."

Without pause and in the same calm voice, Chet added, "Get a good look at them—how many there are, what they're wearing, what they look like. You're going to have to identify them."

There was silence. Someone coughed. At the

commander's word a guerrilla placed a pair of sunglasses on the hostage. Chet asked to retrieve a book from his room. Permission denied. There was no time. He walked to the couch and for a moment held baby Esther who was crying. He kissed three-year-old Anna, turned to Brenda, and asked her to be calm for the girls' sake. A gunman urged him into the rear office.

"Remember," said the policeman, "three hours." He strode from the room with his men. The Ford and van engines started outside. The vehicles pulled away from the house, their noise faded down the street, and Chet was gone.

Train Up a Child . . .

January 20, 1981

His wine glass raised, his imposing figure flanked by marble pillars, the president of the United States addressed the congressional leaders and inaugural participants seated before him at lunch in the resplendent elegance of the Capitol's Statuary Hall.

"With thanks to Almighty God," he began, "I have been given a tag line, the get–off line everyone wants at the end of a toast or speech. Some thirty minutes ago, the planes bearing our prisoners left Iranian airspace and now are free of Iran. We can all drink to this one."

Applause broke from the elated audience.

The picture shrank to a dot on the screen as forty-seven-year-old Chester Bitterman, Jr., flicked off the borrowed TV in despair and began wandering aimlessly through his Lancaster County, Pennsylvania, home. This should be a good day. It should be a great day. The Americans were free, his man Reagan had made it into office, the country would be swinging conservative again—he had waited years for a day like this.

But the victory was bittersweet. Somebody somewhere in that God-forsaken country down there had his son by the throat with a gun at his back. Those Marxists. He was no fool; he had read the magazines. Seemingly isolated acts of terrorism world-wide could, be traced back to a single source if you probed long enough. Moscow exported more blood than vodka.

A wave of nausea and grief engulfed him.

He knew he'd never see his boy again.

If he could he'd get on a boat and go down there and tear that city apart brick by brick till he found young Chet and the vermin holding him. He'd kill them. He'd break their necks or pump them full of holes with a .45.

He wanted to curse. Christians weren't supposed to curse. He thought he would anyway. He hated them!

He half-walked, half-stumbled down the stairs that wound to the basement. He found himself leaning against the door post of what used to be Chet's room, staring inside. There was the bunk bed—you needed bunks with eight kids.

> *Chet*
> *Curt*
> *Connie*
> *Carol*
> *Craig*
> *Chris*
> *and Cindy*

Of course there was Grant, too, after Craig. How a "G" got in there he could never remember.

There were advantages to having eight. Always enough hands to help with the work (heaven knew there was plenty of that to go around). And the nest would never empty out—surely some of the kids would settle close by. There would be grand-children. Best of all, at least a few of the boys would work into the business.

A lump caught in the rugged man's throat. The

family business. Why had Chet left? What was so bad about scale repairs? What was so wrong about staying home to help your father who had raised you since birth?

A brief smile appeared. The kid was sure ugly when he was born. The doctors had to pull him out by the head with forceps because he wouldn't cooperate with his mother. "He doesn't look like much now, but I guess he'll be all right," Mr. Bitterman had told his wife.

As a matter of fact, the boy did turn out all right, a creative, healthy, industrious little charmer with coke-bottle glasses and a carbonated personality.

He reflected on the lad's fondness for his grandmother.

"Could I please have a glass of water, Chetty?" Eager to please, the three-year-old returned a minute later to Grandma's bed, the refreshment in his hand.

"My that's good. Would you get me another sometime?"

Yes, he would. And he did, several times that day. About the third glass, an unsettling suspicion tapped Grandma on the shoulder. She hadn't heard the faucet.

"Chetty, where are you getting it from?"

He looked at her innocently. "The toilet."

An unpleasant taste puckered the mouth of the grinning father. The boy was a charmer all right. It was late December, 1955. Young Chet had received a Bible for Christmas and wanted to read for Grandma. Even at age three he could recite verses and stories remarkably well.

"John 3:16," he said. "I'll huff and I'll puff and have everlasting life." Mr. Bitterman chuckled.

That was twenty-five years ago. He wiped the mist from his eyes, then stepped inside and stretched out on the bed.

Twenty-five years ago. When was that? '55? '56? Was it that long ago? He was still at Trojan Boat in 1956. Children didn't concern him much back then. When he wasn't at work he was helping with church services in trailer parks or handing out Bibles to sailors at the Baltimore harbor . . . or working on cars. He grunted.

Why had Chet turned out so well, he wondered? Or the other kids for that matter? Certainly not because their father had lavished attention on them in their early years. Oh, they tagged along with him to the drag strip and to road rallies. But children didn't interest him then. The boy's warmth came from Mary. His competitive and venturesome spirit . . . . I guess I gave him that, Mr. Bitterman thought. He recalled his own boyhood–exploring storm sewers for miles on end with flashlights, falling twenty feet into a quarry, breaking his knuckles on the jaws of neighborhood kids as he fought his way up the ranks. He didn't recall being afraid, then or hardly ever.

He wondered. Was Chet afraid now?

He tried to picture his son with terrorists, held up in some dirty apartment or perhaps in a makeshift rebel camp out in the jungle. Would Chet try to escape? Would he struggle? Danger had always held a certain fascination for the boy. It fed his competitive spirit—driving him, daring him.

Like his father.

Summer, 1965. A slight breeze toyed with the ripples at the mouth of the Delaware Bay, its lazy swells rocking the Bitterman family boat.

"We'll be up in half an hour," Dad had told them, so Mary, Chet, and the others lounged on the deck, reading and munching in the sun.

Sixty feet below, in wet suits and scuba gear, Mr. Bitterman and his brother continued to drop, expecting to reach bottom within twenty feet. Maybe it was a little crazy diving after treasure in the hulls of sunken sixteenth-century vessels. And true, they hadn't planned ahead much. But Marx's *East Coast Wrecks* said the ships were here. Think of the charities and missionaries they could support with all that gold.

The surface above lifted higher and higher, but the men could not see it. Their underwater lights pierced only eighteen inches into the murky waters, now turned pitch dark by agitated sediment. They had dropped to about one hundred and twenty feet when something knocked their flippers, startling them. Was it a huge fish? By reflex they withdrew their legs. When they eased down a moment later, it happened again.

This time the divers started down head first, their lamps in front of them. In the inky blackness, just inches below his eyes, Mr. Bitterman saw what looked like an enormous sheet of brown sandpaper whirring by at great speed. His nose almost touched it.

He felt dull. His senses weren't serving him well. What was going on? Then he realized. This was the bottom, the ocean floor, and it was moving—fast!

He checked his compass. The bottom was moving west. How could that be? It would run into the land. Wait a minute. The bottom couldn't be going anyplace. It was the water that was moving, and it must be going east. That means we're moving east.

The next place Bitterman knew of to the east was England.

The horrified divers looked at each other and shot for the surface, hardly bothering to decompress. Their heads broke water; they scanned about and saw nothing.

Absolutely nothing.

Hours later twelve-year-old Chet helped pull his exhausted, half-drowned father and uncle out of the Atlantic into a search boat.

"Wow, Daddy, what guts!" the boy said as his father recounted their underwater ordeal. "You're a hero."

On the bottom bunk in his Lancaster County home Mr. Bitterman came back to the present. A hero. To some, his son was a hero now. Did he know it? Did he realize Christians all over the world had gotten word of his capture and were praying for him this instant?

If ever Chet would need his daring and competitive spirit it was now. The boy was caught in a current. His father dreaded to think where it might drag him.

*   *   *

Chester Allen Bitterman III. State: Pennsylvania. Birthdate: November. 30, 1952. Sex: All boy.

Together with Curt, his next oldest brother and closest friend, young Chet adventured, explored, and Tom–Sawyered his way through childhood at a pace that kept his guardian angel working overtime. Riding bikes. Playing ball. Digging forts. Climbing quarries. Breaking collar bones.

The boy rarely came down sick even though he seldom dressed warmly. "Chester Allen Bitterman, did you come to school in shirt sleeves again?" Miss Hartshorne would demand as the rest of the class filed through the door bound in mittens, coats, and boots. Maybe it was the vitamins that kept him healthy. Every morning his mother piled them high in jar lids along the kitchen, counter for each child. Evenings, she would spread out Pennsylvania cooking of inspiring quality and quantity.

Their clothes were dated, their house crowded (five boys shared a tiny bedroom), and their neighborhood a bit run down, but the Bittermans always managed to scrape up enough money for two things—boats and books.

The boats were small and got bigger only as Mr. Bitterman's income increased in later years. But books received a high priority from the beginning.

"My kids aren't going to waste their minds soaking in cartoons and Captain Kangaroo," their father had decided. Minds were like computers: garbage in, garbage out. As a result, the family never owned a television. Instead, children's classics lined racks and shelves all over the house, and the youngsters buried their heads in them. At first, simple, illustrated stories were all they read. But their tastes grew with their, bodies and soon Rudyard Kipling, Arthur Conan Doyle, and Robert Louis Stevenson held their attention hour after hour. All of the children read them, but Chet devoured them.

It was this concern for learning, plus a high regard for religious training, that led the Bittermans to enroll five-year-old Chet in a small Christian school. Here their young scholar could learn important values along with the usual math, spelling, and history. Here, too, he could profit from the classroom discipline.

"Gary Gentle!" Miss Hartshorne's authoritative voice stiffened the class. Her icy gaze and the gesture of her head meant, "Meet me outside." Gary followed his inquisitor, her ruler in her hand, out the door.

Eli Whitney and his cotton gin had failed to capture the fifth grade history class's attention that afternoon. Gary's and Chet's stinging of Carol Ann with a bobby pin had succeeded. Fortunately for Chet, only Gary had been caught. Every ear strained to catch the upcoming showdown in the hall.

Imaginary drum rolls. Whack!

Chester Bitterman thought that was how his muskrat traps would sound on the fingers of any trespasser who dared come crawling into his and Curt's underground fort in the backyard.

He finished the last end-of-the-chapter question, then signed his paper "Abraham Lincoln" as usual. Definitely an A, he judged. His teachers judged that Chet could make all A's if he would take his fun a little less seriously.

"Okay, let's mind our own business and hand in our papers." Miss Hartshorne was back and covering for Gary who returned, beet-faced, to his desk. "You know I love you," she always told them after a whipping; then she hugged them till the sniffles were over. The twinkle was back in her eyes. They knew she did.

* * *

Soda dispensers fizzed, upbeat organ music bounced from the walls, and wooden slats rumbled under the rhythmic churn of skates. Whizzing, shrieking, colliding junior and senior high school students—several hundred of them—churned in a human whirlpool. Rocky Springs Roller Rink's "Youth for Christ Night" was a smash.

Sure-footed skaters in the main flow. glided past the slower-moving novices who stretched their arms on either side for balance like cross beams atop telephone poles. Rednecks with greased hair zoomed backwards, weaving in and out, crossing their feet, bopping to the beat. In the center, prissy girls with skating skirts tried figure eights and backward, one-legged circles.

Along the edge, rarely venturing from the rail, shuffled an ungraceful eighth grader, his shirttail out, his mishaps the single greatest cause of pileups that evening. He stumbled toward the side benches—grinning, oblivious, the incarnation of adolescence.

"Couples only," the announcement came over the speakers. "The next skate is for couples only."

Ceiling lights dimmed and the organ toned down to soft, romantic melodies. A few of the skaters began pairing off and soon a number of hand-holding twosomes stepped onto the floor. Still grinning, Chet Bitterman pushed his glasses off his nose and continued pulling himself along the wall toward the snack bar.

There, handing his nickel over the counter, stood classmate Bradley Hunsaker, obviously not in need of another Hershey Bar. Chet wheeled up beside him.

"I've been talking to Beth Van Ormer," Chet said seriously. "She likes you but she's shy."

Before Bradley could respond Chet was gone, making his way in the semi-darkness through the crowd to a wing where two girls huddled together on a bench. Chet pulled up and parked himself in front of Beth.

"I've been talking to Bradley Hunsaker," he said, sincerity oozing from his face. "He'd like to ask you to skate but he's shy."

Before you could blush and say, "Who, that creep?" he had turned and clattered away.

Eyes rolling, Beth and her friend Vickie headed for the lavatory. How could one person be so together and so out of it at the same time! Everybody liked Chet. They admired his intellect and secretly respected the way he always stood up for the underdog—even for sourpuss Mr. Drescher at school. But his pranks, that crewcut, and those diddly bops–white socks went out with dinosaurs.

They reached the ladies-room and wheeled toward a mirror that was blocked off by a crowd of girls whose mascara hadn't run since the last facial overhaul ten minutes earlier. No one wanted to be caught stranded on the benches halfway through a couple's skate.

"You the girls from Hempfield Shelly brought?" a ladies room debutante asked over the chatter.

"Um, no," said Beth. "I don't know a Shelly."

"No big loss," the girl responded. "She's a little strange anyway. What's your name?"

"Beth. This is my friend Vickie."

"Oh, I know a Vickie. Anyway, I'm Chris. Say, who was that kid with the crewcut talking to you on the bench out there? He nearly wiped me out on the corner. He's not your boyfriend, is he?"

"Are you kidding?" replied Beth. "He's just a guy in our class at school."

"Where do you go?"

Beth and Vickie's eyes met before Vickie answered. "Lancaster Christian Day School."

"Lancaster Country Day?"

The two friends blushed, wishing they did indeed attend the prestigious private academy the girl had just mentioned. Vickie repeated herself.

"No, Lancaster Christian Day School. Our parents send us there."

"Oh, isn't that a reform school or something?" quipped a gum-chewing girl nearby.

The girls held their tongues, but for the umpteenth time that week Beth asked herself why she couldn't attend a *public* school like normal kids, or at least a private school with class. In elementary school the strict rules hadn't mattered that much, or the weekly Bible memory, or having the same teacher for four grades out of six.

But this was junior high. One had one's social dignity to maintain. How could she admit that the elementary school met in that brick monstrosity that had once been a shoe factory? And now things were worse; her class—six kids—was stuck in some church basement. P.E. was held at a public park several blocks away, across the street from the county jail. She and her girl friends just knew the guards on the wall gawked at them as they did calisthenics in those stupid pedal pushers. What a drag—no gymnasium, no sports teams. Just rules.

The whole dress code was senile. Length checks—outrageous! She looked like the only girl in the world who didn't know hemlines were on the way up.

Beth smiled as she wheeled to the mirror. Things were different on weekends. She drifted back to all those Saturdays when she and Vickie had caught the bus into downtown Lancaster. There they would buy gaudy earrings and cheap make-up at Woolworths, duck into the ladies room at Watt & Shands department store, and hem their skirts up with pins. For a few hours they would stroll around town feeling normal until it was time to reassume their everyday identities and go home.

A tap from Vickie returned Beth to the present. She turned and followed her friend out of the lavatory. House lights were bright. ALL SKATE beamed on the neon sign. In the wings they spotted Chet and some noisy friends pulling up on another

35

boy's belt. Chet called the procedure "a snuggie." How crude.

Beth wondered if Chet thought much about girls. She couldn't imagine. Still, she felt sorry for him because when the other kids paired off at school or camp, Chet was always left by himself. Oh, he'll come around, she told herself. Give him another year or two.

∗   ∗   ∗

Forty varsity hopefuls in full uniform puffed and grunted under a blistering August sun to the marine-style barking of football coach Art Grimm.

"Dig it out, dig it out, dig it out!" he roared, the blood vessels on his neck gorged and erect. "Hit the dirt! On your feet! Knees high! Knees high!"

Coach Grimm was well named.

Chet Bitterman pushed up, sat up, and sprinted with his comrades, grinning from ear to ear with delight—the only one on the field apparently enjoying the torture.

"Too slow, you bunch of girls! Four laps around the field. Move it! Move it!"

An exhausted train of bodies plodded around the perimeter.

Joy swept through Chet. Lancaster Christian Day School stopped at ninth grade, and now he'd be playing for Conestoga Valley Public High School. Honest-to-goodness, card-carrying sports, not the second-rate, intramural tiddlywinks they played in junior high. It was a joy to run laps. A privilege.

That afternoon they broke into teams and scrimmaged. Chet stared in awe at the wild and daring exploits of his idol, Dale Scot. Scot kept a wrench in his pants to beat up on rivals during pileups. Who would have thought of it? Could anything be more wonderful?

The boys sprawled on the grass and gasped for breath after a particularly grueling work-out.

"I love it, I love it," Chet spewed between breaths.

"You nuts?" a teammate asked, watching them both drown in sweat.

Chet collected himself, sat erect, and gazed toward the horizon. He looked like a hero in a war movie about to say a stirring line. "I love pain." The melodrama dripped. "I thrive on it. I seek and cherish it as I would a friend."

The teammate rolled his eyes. "Craaaaazy." But before the word was half out Chet had landed on him and applied a head lock with his last ounces of strength, challenging the blasphemer to wrestle.

Everyone soon learned that Bitterman loved to wrestle. It didn't matter if the opponent was a two-hundred-and-twenty-pound, fifth-degree black-belt against whom the sophomore stood no chance—he wanted to wrestle. And he wrestled with a ferocity that caught athletes twice his size by surprise.

Chet returned home dog tired and second string but respected and liked by everyone. And so it was for the next three years.

* * *

Leaning back on slender hips as he stood in front of the mirror, Chet ran a comb one last time through his hair, satisfying himself that every wave was in place. He reached for a flask of cologne and hesitated. Should it be English Leather tonight, or British Sterling? British Sterling—may as well do it right. Glancing down he wished his father hadn't made him take back the alligator leather, pumped-heel shoes he'd come home with the week before. "My sons aren't going to wear Puerto Rican shoes," he had said. Oh well. That was Daddy. On the way out of his room he grabbed his varsity letter jacket and then bounded up the stairs to the dining room where the family was finishing off a meat loaf.

"All set, Daddy."

Mr. Bitterman dug into his pocket and handed over the keys. "I'm telling you, Chet, take it easy. Don't take corners like you're on the cycle."

"Yes sir." With that he was out the door.

Twenty minutes later Beth Van Ormer slid in beside him and together they sped off for Lancaster in Mr. Bitterman's white '57 Ford Fairlane with the fender skirts and torn air-bubble seat covers—their Mach I, Curt and Chet called it. Between conversation Chet tried to calculate how many miles they would put on that night. At ten cents a mile, renting a car from Dad added up quickly.

The Victorian Fulton Opera House seemed out of their class to the young couple standing before its ornate wooden doors. Beth paused. Chet re-membered, grinned, and opened the door. He was learning; she was a good teacher. He surrendered their tickets to the usher who led them down the carpeted aisle to their seats.

"Must be a Bitterman," a male voice said. Turning, they saw one of the boys on Chet's football team, dressed in a suit, seated with his date. The boy smiled. "I told Ann it had to be Curt or Chet. Who else would wear his school jacket to Shakespeare?"

Chet shrugged and they went on.

After the show they dined in a quaint restaurant, laughing, talking, looking very much at home with each other. As the waitress took their dessert orders, Chet engaged the girl in conversation. What is it like to be a waitress? What's the best part about the job? The worst? Do most people tip well? The girl became embarrassed and excused herself.

Beth smiled. That was one thing she liked most about Chet: He was interested in everybody and everything. His questions were the adult equivalent of the endless queries of children, like "What ch'ya doing?" and "How come?"

They discussed their schools, the future, and life. "What do you think it's like to be married, Beth?"

Beth thought, jiggling the ice in her glass. "I don't know. It seems now like it would be great. But that's not the way it is for most of the adults I know."

"Why do you think that is?"

"I don't know."

"You think it's because they didn't find the right person, or because they just didn't work at it hard enough?"

Beth looked at Chet and felt warm inside. She loved the way his mind worked, the things he thought about. "You tell me, Chet."

Chet leaned over the table and looked steadily into her blue eyes. "I think it's because most people didn't care about finding out who God had in mind for them to marry."

"How do you go about finding that?" asked Beth.

"I'm not sure," he said. "Like, how would you and I know if we were cut out for each other in His mind? Still, I don't think God plays guessing games with people. I'll bet—"

A motorcycle with no muffler barreled down the street past their window.

"Did you catch that?" Chet strained his neck to admire the machine.

Beth nodded, grinning.

"I think it was a Harley. I'd love a Harley."

"And the jacket to go with it?"

"Why not?" smiled Chet.

"Oh, you'd go over big, brrroom-brrrooming into Calvary Church parking lot in a leather jacket with your Harley. Headline, *Lancaster New Era*: 'Local Motorcycle Tough Guy Lectures in Church Concerning God's Will for Marriage.' You're an odd combination, buster."

Chet forgot his seriousness. "Look who's talking. Cast the telephone pole out of thine own, eye, sister, before thou searchest for the toothpick in mine. Tsk, tsk, tsk working on the Sabbath selling french fries and the Colonel's chicken."

Beth playfully rose to the challenge. "You think you're so pious 'cause you tote a French New Testament to church."

"There's no French on the cover!"

"Such modesty."

"Tu es fou, mon petit chou."

"No, you're the crazy one."

Chet grasped in vain for a comeback. Quietly they ate their dessert.

"Beth," Chet asked a moment later, not looking up.

"Yeah?" Her voice was soft.

"What's going to happen when we graduate?"

"You mean with us?"

"Yeah, that too, but with our careers, our lives. What do you think it's going to be like in college? And after that, out in the world?"

Neither spoke for a minute.

"Do you think they've fed us a line all these years? Do you think church and Lancaster Christian was just a big plot from our folks to keep us in line? Or do you think—"

"—it's all for real?" Beth concluded his sentence.

"Yeah."

Beth studied Chet's face, knowing they both knew the answer but weren't quite ready to admit it. Of course Christianity was true, and after they'd gotten into public high school they'd found themselves more appreciative of their childhood upbringing than they ever would have thought.

I feel schizophrenic sometimes, Bethy," Chet said, fingering his napkin. "You know I'm going to Columbia Bible College next fall. The 'Bible' part is for my dad's benefit, and a little for mine I guess. The 'college' part is to get away from home."

He paused and looked up at her. "I know I'm a Christian but the things my friends at school do look like so much honkin' fun sometimes."

A smile crossed his face and he slid his hand over hers. "What am I telling you for? You're just the same way."

She smiled in return. "I know. I think that's why we fit so well together."

Four months later Chet and Beth graduated. They spent that summer working, Chet for his dad and Beth as an Amish country tour guide, snatching all the spare hours they could with their families, boating on the river. But August came and went, and with it the joys and freedoms of high-school life. September inched onto the calendar, and the two parted with a tender good-by, Beth for Houghton College in New York state, and Chet for the deep South in search of a little education and as much tomfoolery as possible.

A Little Education

The campus of Columbia Bible College sweltered in the South Carolina heat of early September 1970. But like a prim southern belle, she perspired with dignity. Not a soda can or candy wrapper disgraced her lawns. Not a word of graffiti marred her elegant brick.

Like hundreds of students before him, Chet wondered what the school would hold for him. Would it be a four-year playground? Or the spark that would set his Christianity aflame? He should know soon enough.

"Are you guys returning students?" Chet asked the boys beside him his first evening in the cafeteria. Getting no response he realized with embarrassment that they had closed their eyes and were praying for their food.

"Sorry," he mumbled when they had finished.

"No problem," they assured him. The boys introduced themselves and welcomed him to Columbia. Chet began to think this was not a bad place.

The sophomores were clearly glad to be together again. Warm reunions among returning students had been going on all day. Even there in, the cafeteria bear hugs and back slapping continued as friends saw each other for the first time that year.

Looking around the tile-floor room, Chet saw that Columbia drew a wide diversity of people—country boys, jocks, foreign students, eggheads, pretty girls, plain Janes, even Southern rebels still fighting the war. Fashion conscious young people sprinkled the room: girls in stylish dresses, boys with crisp new bell bottoms and every hair in place—Sears catalog types. Chet guessed that some of the older students who had been through the military didn't realize they could grow their hair out again. One of them inched past Chet's table in the dinner line a few feet away. He seemed to be studying a small packet of cards pulled from his shirt pocket.

"I've seen several guys with those," Chet said to the boys at his table. "Are they trying to get a jump on a course or something?"

"No, they're verse packs," a Georgia boy answered.

"Bible verses?"

"Yeah, on those little cards."

"For a course?"

"Nuh-uh," the sophomore shook his head. "He's a Navigator."

"Nagrivator," someone at the table corrected, dryly.

Chet smiled, confused. "What's the deal?"

"You've heard of nicotine fits?" the Georgian asked.

Chet nodded.

"Well, these guys get verse fits." He acted out his words. "Every so often when the urge gets strong Navs reach for their verse packs, grab one of those little babies out and—ahh! Good for another ten minutes."

The table broke into laughter.

"Navigators, Chet," one of them explained, "is an organization that works with college students and military guys. It gets them sharing their faith and memorizing Scripture. I had a brother in the Air Force—got his life turned around through Navs. They're pretty committed to what they're studying and doing." He pointed to the others and added in mock confidentiality, "These guys have sour grapes because they're afraid they couldn't handle it."

Bah's of protest.

Chet grinned. He didn't think memorizing verses would appeal to him either.

They dropped into conversation about their families, their backgrounds, and the college. As the sophomore described the first-year courses, Chet found himself suddenly staring into the boy's belt buckle. All of the non-freshmen at the table had quickly risen to their feet for two approaching women students.

Quite the gentlemen, Chet thought, standing as well. "Glad to meet you." The table had barely been seated when one of the girls, looking as if she had forgotten something, got up from her chair and started off. The boys stood again. In a moment she returned with a glass of milk. Up again. Chet guessed this was the only cafeteria in the world where you weighed less when you left than when you came in. He had a lot to learn.

> Dear Beth,
>
> The campus is really beautiful. The buildings are all brick and everything is air-conditioned, except the dorms and cafeteria. . . . Everyone is more or less your friend here.
>
> This morning one teacher invited any of the boys up to his house any time at all for a milk shake. . . . I don't know what else I'll learn, but I believe that I'll really get to know God a lot better. . . . The college has a lot of emphasis on missions. I don't know what I'll turn out to be yet.

Night had fallen, though not the temperature, and Chet's handwriting became sloppy as his eyelids grew heavy. He told Beth he missed her then signed the letter, Lots of love, Chet.

"Chet?"

"Yeah, Dave?" Chet's roommates were trying to sleep.

"Do you play drums in a band or something? Stop tapping your pen."

"Sorry man." He snapped off the light and went to bed.

The next several days held few dull moments for

freshmen, being packed with get-acquainted socials and orientation meetings. A new student at Columbia needed plenty of orientation.

"Here at CBC we have one objective," a grandfatherly faculty member began in a southern drawl. He pointed to the school motto embossed in steel letters on the front chapel wall: TO KNOW HIM AND TO MAKE HIM KNOWN. "Everything goes toward reaching that goal."

Tim Thompson, a freshman from Michigan, leaned forward in his twelfth row seat, deeply interested. On page nine of his comic book, Flash Gordon was about to ray-gun a Wan-Deji alien into oblivion on the planet Narzuma. He hated to do it, but that's what happens when someone sabotages your astro-gyro flight-path stabilizer. Tim brushed the bangs from his eyes and turned the page.

Chet's gaze momentarily left the podium and drifted to his friend's lap. He wasn't sure what it was about Tim he liked so much. Crazy dude.

The tail end of a sentence from the podium caught Chet's attention. Something about two hours' cleaning a week to keep tuition down. He decided he had better listen. He wanted to listen.

"Now about church," the speaker said. "We have enough churches in this town to entertain you with something new for years to come if that's what you want. But church-hopping is no good. Sunday morning smorgasbord keeps you from developing meaningful relationships with Christians off campus. So, we expect you to pick one church and stick with it throughout your college years.

The lecturer went on to explain the Christian service requirement. Each student would be assigned five hours weekly of teaching a Sunday school class, working in jails, helping juvenile delinquents, or taking care of some similar responsibility. This would give students experience and keep them from becoming a "holy huddle," out of touch with life.

Chet grunted. This place meant business. He appreciated the faculty explaining the rationale behind the rules. They had thought things through.

The assembly adjourned and each freshman received a copy of the Student Handbook on his way out. Chet arrived at the dorms a few minutes behind his roommates. Fred, a Florida boy with wire-rimmed glasses who resembled Elton John, lay plopped on his bunk listening to a Beatles album. Across the room Dave was straightening out his desk.

A knock came on their door, and two boys entered without waiting for an answer—Tim, who had sat beside Chet in the chapel, and his buddy, Mike.

Tim waved his rule book. "Did you guys read this thing yet?"

Chet lit up. "Hey, Timbo."

Tim ignored Chet's greeting and posed his question again. Had they read the joke book? Pardon him, the rule book? "What is this, some kind of Christian boot camp? These guys think they're going to get us out of bed at 6: 15 every morning."

"Where does it say that?" asked Fred in disbelief.

"Right here," answered Mike, pointing to the page. "Six fifteen. But that's nothing. Checkout the other stuff. "

The boys dived into their copies.

"Catch page twenty-six." Tim read aloud. "Dress shirts and ties are to be worn at all weekly evening meals and at Sunday dinner."

Chuckles and oh-brothers.

"Men students' hairlines are to be above the eyes, off the ears, and above the collars."

Laughter.

"Faithful application of biblical principles rules out the use of rock music or jazz on campus."

Raucous laughter.

"Students must absolutely avoid holding hands, embracing, kissing, and other physical contacts." Whoops, cat calls, pounding on the desks.

The rules specified that students could date only on weekends and then only so many hours per week on a graduated scale from one's freshman to senior year.

"What the fat are you supposed to do between weekends–monk it?" asked Fred.

"Whoa," said Chet. "The turbulent storms of youthful love and passion no longer lie dormant in the heart of young Frederick."

"Back off Bitterman," Fred retorted. "You don't have anything to worry about; you've got that woman on the string back home."

"I'll tell you what you do on weekdays," interrupted Tim. "Marlita told me. You don't date." He put his nose in the air and fluttered his eyelids. "You socialize."

"Ooh," the boys answered in unison, cocking their little fingers and pretending to hold tea cups.

"Excuse my ignorance," said Dave, "but what's that?"

"You'll find out this week at supper when the

rules go into effect." Tim threw his book down. "Mike and I are gonna cruise off campus and breathe for awhile. Anyone coming?"

Life settled in over the next several weeks. Chet was assigned to the Rikard Nursing Home ministry for his Christian service. Each Tuesday a dozen or so students held chapel for the residents, then visited room to room.

On Sundays the students descended upon the city's churches. As the ten-week deadline to settle on one congregation drew near, the new students increased the busy pace of their sampling. Crowded into the cars of the few freshman fortunate enough to own them, the first year students discussed their choices to and from church: First Baptist, Covenant Presbyterian, Columbia Evangelical, Donut Baptist....

"Donut Baptist?" Everyone stared at their driver.

"Yeah. You know. Bodie's church. They whip out pastries and Coke in college-age Sunday school."

True enough, since Columbia was a college town most of the churches made special efforts to welcome students. But donuts and the red-carpet treatment failed to interest Chet. "Tonight," he wrote Beth,

> I went to a very small, dumpy, black church down in the poor side of town. This church is held in an old building like a fire hall and there's only about 50-75 people that go

there—about 90-95% of these are kids and are they rowdy! I don't know for sure if I'll choose this church but it sure can use teachers.

Sunday morning. Six weeks into the semester.

"Say, Chet." A voice from a Chevrolet window called to the Pennsylvanian who had just stepped from the dorms onto the parking lot. "Want to check out Waverly Street Methodist?"

Chet smiled but waved them on. A minute later Tim rumbled up in his Plymouth Sport Fury. Chet got in.

"How'd you talk me into this, Bitterman?"

"Aw, Tim m'boy." He shut his door and winked. "These little kids'll love you." Tim rolled his eyes, gunned the engine, and sped out for the fire hall.

* * *

For the first day that month the out-of-doors managed a genuine October feel. Sweater weather. It was a bright, blustery afternoon with cotton clouds that lost no time in traveling across the sky.

Wop!

A goalie's kick sent the soccer ball a hundred feet into the air. Ooh's rose from several hundred spectators on the grassy slopes. An away game against the University of South Carolina was big time for a small private school with only one intercollegiate sport.

Chet watched enviously the graceful moves of athletes on both teams. Before this year he had hardly ever kicked a ball. Now he played for the freshman intramural team. He hoped to play for the school team before long.

Like the other Bible college students, Chet wore blue jeans. Blue jeans were allowed on Saturday, and everyone took advantage of the privilege. He glanced around at some of the university students. Blue jeans. Long hair. A few beards.

Chet liked beards. He liked long hair, too. Not down on the shoulders like Frank Zappa, just long enough to hide one's ears. By now most of the Bible college boys had succumbed to the barber's razor. A few just plastered their hair back on the sides so they could comb it down again whenever studying at the university library.

For many CBC students an aura surrounded university kids. They studied at a real school, a secular school. The word "secular" attracted and intimidated at the same time. It carried images of ivy-covered lecture halls, student sophistication, and unquestioned academic status. But could a Christian survive on such a campus? Could he hold his own in discussion with an informed skeptic? Belief in the biblical accounts of Jonah and Noah seemed naive beside an urbane secularism.

For the life of him Chet could not relate to such fears. Not anymore. Not that he had all of life's answers or that Columbia had no second-rate courses. Every school had a few. But for the most part he couldn't be more impressed.

Take Mr. Supplee, the choir director—there he sat on the sidelines, cheering and hollering. Every September the former USO entertainer determined to teach each of his students—even those tone deaf like Chet—to sight-read and lead congregational singing by year's end. He usually succeeded.

Then there was his Old Testament lecturer, the Australian archaeologist who had conducted digs in Palestine. Wilson knew his material. He had authored two of the course texts.

Of course, there was Doc Fortosis, President McQuilkin, and the venerable Hatch. But Chet's favorite course was Bible Introduction where the professor—a short, red-headed scholar who talked as fast as he thought—argued convincingly for the historical reliability of the New Testament.

"To begin with, how do we know we have the New Testament substantially as it was written?' he had asked the class. "How do we know it hasn't been tampered with over the centuries? To ask that question you must also ask the same for the works of Livy and Aristotle and other ancient writers. For the historical reliability of the gospels is tested by the same principles that test all historical documents. The following are the three basic principles of historiography . . . ."

Pens scribbled furiously as the animated instructor launched the class into the world of textual criticism. Unearthed copies of Caesar's Gallic War competed that afternoon for respectability alongside the manuscripts of the Greek New Testament. Replicas of the Annals of Tacitus, eight hundred years removed from the original work, stood before the bar next to the parchments of the Apostles.

Lost originals and the age of their surviving copies suddenly grew fascinating. Yellowed scrolls and brittle papyrus fragments paged their way into the twentieth century. Students drank in the results of paleographical dating. Thucydides, Herodotus, the great Roman historians—all had their day in court.

Then the great museums and university libraries of the world marshaled their collected manuscripts of the New Testament writings. Four thousand documents they produced, in Greek alone.

Caesar blushed with his dozen.

Tacitus winced at the antiquity of the biblical documents.

"The manuscript evidence for the New Testament is vastly superior to that of the classical writings," the professor concluded. "Although the original documents are lost, we have so many copies of such high value that 99.5 percent of the original text of the New Testament has been reconstructed through the science of textual criticism. Only one-half of a percent of the New Testament text is in doubt, and at these points of doubt we have slightly different readings from the different manuscripts from which to choose."

Chet and his fellow students had been impressed with these and other arguments—with the archaeological evidence, the historical witnesses, the scholars who had spent their careers trying to disprove the resurrection of Jesus only to become convinced themselves in the face of the evidence.

How different this was from Chet's high-school impression of the Christian faith as something to be apologized for. He needn't shelve his brains when opening his Bible.

* * *

The halls of Columbia Bible College were not always the inner sanctums of order and piety they appeared to be from the outside. Somehow dead fish spontaneously generated in the grad assistant's toilet, soda cans hurled themselves down the halls during quiet hours and lighted matches found their way to Right Guard-soaked tops of overturned trash cans.

"I have many memories about Chet," Steve Sprunger, his floor leader, wrote years later. "Some good, some maybe not so good. Shortly after he started living on my floor I realized that if there was trouble, it was usually in his room, and he was in the middle of it."

The object of many assorted pranks was Bob Kallgren, Dorm Six's graduate assistant who, for all his friendliness, was kept at arm's length by Chet. "Hey, hey, hey, Bobby K.," Chet addressed him, and the tag stuck for years. Bob thought he sensed in Chet an occasional urge for serious discussion, but the authority gap apparently stood too wide to bridge.

Late one night some pandemonium upstairs awakened Bob in his first-floor room. He could guess the source. The graduate assistant sprang up and sprinted down the hall. He would crash through the swinging wooden door at the corridor's end, scale the steps, and nab the offenders. A piano behind the door stopped him dead. Not even the punishment meted out the next morning by the dorm council could squelch Chet's delight over his successful stratagem.

Bob encouraged Steve Sprunger, the upstairs floor leader, to turn Chet in more often. "If I had followed this advice every time Chet broke the rules his first six months at CBC," wrote Steve, "I'm sure he would have been expelled. I really can't say why I didn't turn him in to Dean

Braswell more often, but something (or Someone) seemed to keep me from doing so."

Sometimes no one had to turn Chet in. "Something bothering you, man?" asked Tim. Chet had steered him into an empty laundry room.

"Yeah, I've got to talk to you." Chet's face was pale.

"Well, what is it?"

"Tim, I . . . I just don't know how it happened, but . . . well . . . I kissed Janie Beard behind the chapel. Tim blinked as if expecting more. When he realized there was no more he grinned. Then he laughed. "Is that all? Whoo! Janie Beard behind the chapel." He doubled over. "So what's the big deal? You've laid a smacker on Beth Van Ormer before."

Chet's expression didn't change. "That was different. I wasn't breaking a rule."

Nothing Tim could say deterred Chet from turning himself in to the dean. the next day and receiving a work penalty.

This serious, conscience-sensitive side of Chet—a side few people saw—impressed itself on Steve Sprunger as the "real" Chet.

> I just could not get away from the fact that under all the outside mischief, Chet was a valuable person. Chet would sometimes come to my room and talk from the heart. One night he came and asked me how I knew the Lord was calling me into missionary work. He had a lot of questions about exactly what the "call" was and about my own experience. I guess maybe it was these heart-searching talks with Chet that kept me from turning him in more often. Perhaps I

saw that underneath all the mischievousness, Chet was actually a man longing to serve the Lord.

At opposite ends of the Bible college campus, two hundred yards apart, sat the men's and women's dormitories. Linking them was an arrow-straight sidewalk, the artery between throbbing hearts across the campus.

Every evening at about 5:25, a hundred or more men packed in and around the central women's lobby. Some stood, some paced, some sat in the lounge chairs and skimmed newspapers, but a tie around each neck bound them together.

The bell rang and a hundred or so women, all of them in dresses, sallied out from behind doors and hallways.

The evening's socializing had begun.

Non-socializers quickened their pace to avoid the string of students that now sauntered to the cafeteria in Noah's ark fashion. For the twosomes, a casual stroll up faculty row after dinner would be in order. Since there was little else to do and virtually no other place to congregate, these casual strolls were almost always, in order.

Soon, everyone knew, the 7:00 bell must ring. At that time the men would see their ladies off at the lobby under the gaze of most everyone in the world, then file back across the sidewalk toward their own dorms, pulling off neckties and losing just a trace of their gentility.

"Bottled romance," Chet said to the cooks as he looked out the kitchen window where he worked.

"Makes me glad I work suppers. The whole thing reminds me of those Soft Touch cards."

"You don't like them, Chet?" one of the ladies smiled.

"Oh, I do, I do," he answered. "Especially the ones with a misty photo in front and the message inside that says 'Us.'" His eyes widened. The women laughed.

Chet turned from the window and grabbed a stack of dishes. He was glad to have landed this job, and it showed. He never walked; he ran. The others drew energy just watching him hustle serving trays and manhandle milk dispensers. His laughter and friendliness permeated the kitchen.

Often, students leaving dirty trays and silverware at the dish pit would be attacked by Chet's "African anaconda gaboon viper"—an arm dipped in grease and left-over food slithering up over the counter top.

"Settle down now," Mr. Leavel, the food services' manager, would tell him.

Two sophomore girls who worked in the cafeteria became especially close to Chet. Seeing his peg-legged pants and general ineptness in fashion, these surrogate mothers made him their personal project.

"Chet, what's with those green socks?"

"What's the matter? They match my shirt." He had tried hard.

"You're not back fixing scales in some farmer's barn," they would chide. "We're going to have to fix you up."

A smirk crossed his face. "Well, well," he replied, beginning one of his ridiculous strings of words that ended only when he ran out of breath.

"It's not every day that a young lad stumbles upon such generous offers of help from two lovely young lasses such as yourselves, whose great beauty and charm is exceeded only by your overtures of assistance to the needy."

A nervous laugh came from behind the chuckling girls.

"Chet, you're too much," a slightly built freshman employee, trying to compose himself, said in a thick New England accent. David Tosi's small stature and lack of self-confidence would have disqualified him from the average high school's "Most likely to succeed" list.

"Come on Tosi, you pot-licker," Chet joked. "Let's cut the laughter and frivolity."

David laughed all the harder.

"Tosi, my man, Mr. Leavel wants a reasonable amount of professionalism in this establishment," Chet said, grinning. Then he tickled David. "Settle down."

"I can't," David screamed, splitting his sides and turning red in the face. People began to stare. "Oh my boy, let me help you." Chet pretended to help David with his tray of dishes but instead tormented him under the arms all the more.

"That's enough, Chet!" Mr. Leavel strode in clapping his hands loudly as if hammering a gavel. The scene broke up.

"Tosi must despise Chet," a girl in line whispered to one of Chet's "mothers."

"Despise him?" She smiled, watching the boys resume their duties. "They're going to room together next year."

* * *

Chet's spiritual life limped along his freshman year like a car with dirt in its lines. On the one hand, many of his letters home expressed a desire for maturing faith or included Scripture quotes. On the other hand, the diet of chapel speakers, Bible studies, and prayer groups that nourished him one week choked him the next. "Down here everyone is so much more spiritual or something," he wrote to Beth, "and I feel like a heel that doesn't even belong."

Older, more serious students agreed. His brash conduct and borderline adherence to the regulations (Chet occasionally showed up for coat-and-tie affairs in an old army jacket and clown-suit necktie) made them question why he had ever come. Curt Bitterman visited Chet one weekend in the spring and left with the same impression most people had of his brother—a shallow, fun-and-games man.

Interestingly enough, it was the rowdy crowd at school that knew better. None of them had the slightest doubt where Chet's loyalties lay. Chet might sneak up the off-limits water tower with them, but he wouldn't sneak off campus to down a few beers. He had his convictions—however arbitrary— and he stuck with them.

"And he never condemned me," Tim said of Chet years later. "He let us know where he stood, but he didn't keep us at arm's length as if we'd contaminate him. Sometimes he'd tramp out to the woods behind the dorms with a few of us rebels. We'd have a smoke there—everyone but Chet—and talk about everything under the sun. We never talked theology or anything. But it was obvious from the things Chet said, and just from the way he was, that he loved God. Even at age seventeen, I think Chet was the most God-minded man I ever met."

Early second semester Tim left Columbia, tired of the rules and the penalties for breaking them. For Chet this marked a turning point. Sure there were a lot of rules, he reasoned. But they had a purpose. Besides, were they all Tim and the others could see? Wasn't becoming better acquainted with God worth some unexpected sacrifices?

Slowly, imperceptibly to most, the seeds of Chet's childhood began to germinate. But not till that summer could the shoots be seen poking through the soil.

. . . And When He Is Old

Half a dozen Amish carpenters waited on the steps outside the workshop of Agri, Inc., near Lancaster, Pennsylvania. Sitting next to a row of lathered horses and unhitched buggies, they kept a lookout for their driver. Soon "Jehu" barreled up, namesake of the Old Testament Israelite renowned for the furious handling of his chariot team. No sooner had the plain folk buckled in than the van squealed out of the parking lot, its white-knuckled passengers clutching the arm-rests. My zeidt! The man was crazy.

When it came to a day's labor, however, the Amish had only respect for Jehu. He worked hard up on those barn trusses for somebody "English," even if by lunch he could barely unpry his fingers from the hammer.

"What for morning did you have, Chester?" they would ask in their Pennsylvania Dutch accents, thumbs in suspenders, smiling at his fatigue.

"Oh baby," Chet would grin. "Body thrives on pain."

One summer week the Agri crew raised a dairy barn southwest of Lancaster. Chet was fascinated by the silo builders nearby—energetic men who put in long, feverish hours constructing the storage towers. the faster they worked the more they earned, but the height and absence of safety equipment made the job dangerous.

One of the workers, a college student, explained that he accepted the pace and risks only to earn quick money for the following semester's tuition. Chet nodded; he, too, was a student. Casually, Chet brought up religion. Had the boy read the Bible or thought much about God? The conversation stiffened and Chet dropped the subject. At five o'clock Chet left with the barn-building crew. Fifteen minutes later the silo worker slipped and fell to his death.

That Saturday morning Chet, as usual, ate breakfast with his friend Rob Musser. Like other Saturdays they would spend the day on motorcycles in search of what they called their "cheap thrills." Perhaps they would swim out into the Susquehanna River and leap from an abandoned electrical tower, or bike through lands peppered with "No Trespassing" signs that held promise of unusual sights or encounters with angry landowners. But on this day Chet was solemn. He told Rob of the silo worker's death.

"He was getting ready to go back to school next week, Muss, just like us."

Rob nodded. The boys munched on their cornflakes.

"What runs through your mind when you think about being a lawyer the rest of your life?" asked Chet.

"Oh, I think I'll enjoy solving legal problems," replied Rob. "But I'd like a chance to work with my hands too."

Chet didn't seem to be listening.

"Why?" said Rob. "Where do you think you'll end up? I see you in something a little more intellectual than framing up barns for Agri."

Chet thought a moment. "Rob, when I get to the end of my life, I want to point to something I did that really counted. Thinking about that guy who fell reminds me that this life isn't all there is. I mean, people live forever, Muss . . . one place or another."

The boys stared at each other.

"I may end up working with my hands the rest of my life," said Chet. "But if I do, it'll be to put bread on the table, that's all. I'll always consider my real life's work to be with people."

After breakfast they prayed. They prayed for the silo worker's family and for their own futures. Chet prayed like he talked, respectfully, but as if addressing a close friend.

No artificial sweeteners, thought Rob. Why can't I pray like that?

✷ ✷ ✷

Chet roomed with David Tosi his sophomore year. Apart from his pulling back the curtains whenever Dave got dressed, the unlikely pair did fine. Greek, psychology, literature, and theology claimed most of Chet's time. Still, he found time to play on the soccer team, work with reform-school boys, and pen letters by the score. His performance as a singer depended on whether he was in concert with the college choir (Mr. Supplee had done his job) or in his room singing and dancing on the bed to the records of Seals and Crofts.

The next two summers he worked for his father. Each autumn he was back at school, becoming more serious in his studies, less serious about Beth.

Typically one could spot Chet be-bopping down the sidewalk in an Amish hat, or hunched over a cafeteria table discussing Calvinism or the Vietnam war. He mingled freely. No one group could claim him, but he seemed especially drawn toward social down-and-outers.

His junior year Chet served as student body vice president. His roommate, a freshman, never knew it till November: Chet was as reserved about his achievements as he was private about his love life (which, throughout most of his time at Columbia, did not exist). All through Chet's last three years he and his roommates prayed together nightly. The muscular Pennsylvanian moved easily between wrestling and study, laughter and dialogue, soccer and prayer.

Somehow between his freshman and senior years, Chet grew into a man. He would always praise Columbia for its part in shaping his life, and he generously supported the school until his death. But the lion's share of influence he ascribed to his parents—the kindness of his mother and the rugged discipline of his father.

The morning of September 20, 1973, was one of those times of discipline. It was 9:30 in Lancaster, Pennsylvania.

"York Stone and Supply," his dad said, sticking his head into Chet's bedroom. "Curt's out, I'm tied up. We've gotta have you."

Chet dropped a pair of socks into the empty suitcase and drove to the asphalt plant. He wanted to finish the job quickly so he would have time to pack and get to bed at a decent hour. He'd be pulling off for his senior year of college the next morning.

He strode into the sweltering plant and stared up at the monster vats, four stories high, a hopper beneath them with capacity for ten thousand pounds of sizzling aggregate.

"There it is. Fix it." The manager made clear by his clock-watching and curtness that every minute's delay was costing his shut-down plant an incalculable sum.

Looking like the world's greatest expert, Chet climbed the twenty-eight stairs to the catwalk and surveyed the elaborate measuring device.

"Well? How long is this going to take?"

"I'll call you when it's ready." Chet replied with a calmness he didn't feel.

"You won't need to," said the manager.

Chet spent an hour checking frequent trouble spots. No broken support rods, no stones in the bearings. He spent a second, frequently interrupted hour, calibrating the dial. *No, I'm not done. Yes, I'll send for you the minute it's finished.*

By the time Chet got to the lever system he realized he was in trouble. The manager snorted behind him.

"Hold on. I'm checking." Chet's mind scampered. He toyed busily with the pivots. *Where are those adjustments?* "Maybe it's the Benson release," he said to the manager. "It'll take some time to check."

There was no such thing as a Benson release. A sick feeling settled in Chet's stomach. He needed time. He needed to call his dad on this one—he had never seen a scale like this in his life. But how could he call dad, who felt that asking for help was the height of femininity? Dad would want him to gut it out, to learn by experience.

The following hours in that 100-degree pressure cooker were among the most miserable of Chet's life. In a rage the manager called Mr. Bitterman, and over the phone the three of them figured out where the adjustments were.

That problem solved, Chet hand-carried his two-thousand pounds of test weights up to the hopper and began adjusting and readjusting the levers—

matching them at two-thousand pound increments with the dial, placing and removing the weights a score of times.

At nine that night Chet collapsed in his room, drenched with sweat, still needing to pack. Bitter and frustrated, he caught his dad's figure in the doorway from the corner of his eye. "How did the job turn out?" Mr. Bitterman asked.

Chet recounted the incident with dispassion. "I really appreciate what you did today." His father looked at the floor. "I knew you were in a tight spot but I knew you could handle it." Mr. Bitterman paused awkwardly. "It was a good job, Chet," he said. "Thanks."

For the first time he could remember, Chet felt a lump in his throat over his father. Dad hadn't mentioned his slip-ups or lectured about how he should have handled it. Nor had he taken the opportunity to berate him about his hair length again. He had said thanks.

Chet began throwing T-shirts into his suitcase. Some hurts were healing.

* * *

There had been nothing flashy about the chapel speaker or his manner that rainy spring morning in 1974. He introduced himself as a linguist with Wycliffe Bible Translators, an organization working with over six hundred ethnic groups in twenty-five countries around the world whose purpose it was to translate the New Testament into every language on earth.

"I need a volunteer," he said, "someone from the audience whose native tongue is not English and, preferably, non-Indo-European." A Japanese graduate student came forward and for the next forty-five minutes the animated linguist pointed to the floor, ceiling, parts of the body, and whatever else he could find and motioned for her to name them. He would imitate her sounds and when she seemed satisfied with his reproductions would record them on a blackboard using characters from the international phonetic alphabet.

By chapel's end he had scribbled several blackboards full of nouns, adjectives, verbs, and a few simple phrases.

"That's what a linguist-translator does his first day on the job," the linguist concluded, "provided he can find an informant and doesn't get shot through with arrows." Laughter. "About three thousand ethnic groups still lay tucked away in obscure places around the world. They've never seen their language written nor heard a verse of Scripture. They need someone. Would you consider helping them? Thank you."

The audience applauded and chapel was dismissed. That evening as Chet and his roommate sat at their desks, Chet fidgeted with his pencil stub.

"Did you see that guy in chapel today, Kirk?"

"Yeah."

"I think that's the kind of thing I'd like to do."

"Translate, you mean?"

"Yeah," he said, looking up. "Translate."

Three months later Chet stood on the chapel steps with a degree in his hand and a vivid memory of the linguist's demonstration. "I would like to graduate as an intelligent young man with a good knowledge of the Bible," he had written in his application four years earlier. And now he had. His next twelve months were already planned—he'd be counseling teenagers on a bike tour in Europe that summer, then going home to work for his dad. But for the first time he was fairly sure what he wanted to do with his life.

He had no idea what he was getting into.

The Movement of April Nineteenth

A continent away, twenty-one hundred miles south of Columbia Bible College, a cadre of social activists sat plotting a series of escapades with far more at stake than a dean's office lecture or a Saturday work penalty.

Their thoughts were on a country, not a campus.

Most of them preferred the political route to their objectives. They had tried it. One of their own men, Carlos Toledo Plata, had sat in parliament. Every month, it seemed, he had presented ideas to the legislature. New ideas, good ideas. Suggestions for jobs, plans for health, projects for education.

It had gotten them nowhere. The few and the rich said no. The respectable and powerful said no. The greedy leaders of the so-called democracy said no. Blind pigs.

They were convinced: Colombia was run by pigs.

Their beloved Colombia. For over a century its mountains and plains had been a stage for bloodletting squabbles between liberals and conservatives. They'd been at each other's throats' since the 1830s and what had it gotten the country? Twelve separate constitutions and over twenty civil wars.

On paper, the group agreed, the liberals were right. Liberals opposed making gods of the clergy and maintaining the ridiculous class privileges.

They pressed for universal suffrage; that was good. It was all good theory but it never went far enough. The ones in power were too comfortable on their sprawling ranches and in their plush suburban homes. None of them had the guts to do much.

Until Gaitan. Now there was a man.

Jorge Eliecer Gaitan. His opponents had railed him as a dreamer, but for Colombia's hungry and unemployed in the late 1940s, such dreams nourished hope. The country could have used a dozen Gaitans, visionaries who could foresee a fair, peaceful, yes, socialist Colombia. A people's democracy.

As the activists saw it, democracy was a joke in Colombia. The nation's president in the late forties had been weak—a mere puppet of the fanatic conservative Gomez who had government police combing the countryside, terrorizing liberals into staying away from the polls in the coming elections. Gaitan· had stood up to Gomez. He had armed the liberal villages and infused their hearts with courage. They, in turn, had stood up, too. No wonder the people loved Gaitan. No wonder they worshiped him.

No wonder his enemies killed him.

They shot him on April 9, 1948—shot the man who was a shoo-in as Colombia's next president. They took his life in a downtown section of the nation's capital, just outside the Nieto Building. A crowd gathered. When they realized who had fallen, disbelief turned to horror, then rage. They found the assassin hiding nearby. Knocking him to the pavement they clawed and kicked as someone bludgeoned him to death with a shoe-shine box.

With a necktie they dragged his naked corpse up Bogota's main street to the presidential palace, yelling, "Death to Gomez!"

The news swept through the city streets setting loose an avalanche of antigovernment destruction. Frenzied mobs overturned streetcars, vandalized offices, and set fire to the presidential palace and other municipal buildings. Flames lit the sky that evening and three days later fires were still smoldering.

Looters and Communists joined in the melee for their own reasons. The shooting and window-shattering spread to stores and private homes. In less than a week three hundred lay dead.

But it was only the beginning. The powder keg had ignited. The violence had begun.

La Violencia. For eighteen years it ebbed and flowed. Whole towns were massacred by men of the opposite party. At times they shot and mache-ted each other at the rate of a thousand per week.

And what did the establishment do? Set up a power-sharing monopoly. Four years the liberals would rule, four years the conservatives—back and forth for twenty years. It was designed to satisfy both parties and stop the violence. They called their plan the National Front. Social dissidents called it the National Joke. For them it was a travesty—a political Band-aid when surgery was needed, a passing of the keys from right pocket to left of the same body: the rich, the powerful, the guardians of the status quo.

But the plan had almost ruptured. April 19, 1970—Colombia's presidential elections. The liberals were bowing out, the conservatives moving in. The "official" conservative candidate was supposed to have had an open-and-shut victory handed him. Everything was set. Both sides agreed.

But the National Front hadn't counted on Rojas. General Gustavo Rojas Pinilla—returned from exile, popular with the peasants, hated by the elite. The swelling of his ranks with known Communists and anti-establishment types made the high and mighty bristle. They hated and feared the way his daughter sold produce on the streets at half price, promising the buyers, "This is what it will cost once we get into power." They despised the way he had conveniently become a splinter conservative for the elections.

Rojas, a conservative. It was a laugh. Everyone knew he was his own man. But it was no laughing matter for conservatives when the polls closed the evening of April 19 and early returns showed Rojas in the lead. The outgoing president announced that the close vote would take several days to tally.

"Fraud!" screamed Rojas's followers.

When the party man was later declared winner by a narrow margin, Rojas's followers did more than scream. Incensed voters swarmed Bogota's streets, clashing with riot squads and bringing martial law down upon themselves. The rioting ended two days later, but not the tension.

Nor the planning.

It was, in fact, that April 19th election that had spawned the group of social activists who sat plotting in a room twenty-one hundred miles south of Columbia Bible College. They had tried to work within the system and had had enough. They would have no more rhetoric, no more rigged elections. They would have action.

The movement of April Nineteenth, they called

themselves. M-19 for short. Their goal was simple: democracy and justice in Colombia. Their methodology would depend on how things went.

"Wait for M-19" the ads in the paper had said.

"M-19 is Coming." People didn't know whether to expect a new floor wax or a brand of cigarettes. They found out soon enough.

January 19, 1974. The sword of Simon Bolivar—nineteenth-century Latin American liberator—disappears from the Bolivar museum. Claiming responsibility: A group calling themselves the M-19 who say the government did not deserve to keep it.

Soon afterwards the premises of Bogota's Municipal Council are occupied by a group known as the M-19. The perpetrators issue political statements.

The following two years. Armed assailants commandeer an occasional milk truck and distribute its contents, free of charge, in poor neighborhoods. Compliments of M-19.

The strategy had worked to a point. Some human rights violations had been exposed, some repression spotlighted. But it wasn't enough. The elite had tried to ignore them. "Idealistic young Robin Hoods" the establishment called them. "Dedicated amateurs with a flair for derring-do."

Dedicated they were. But not amateurs. They knew what they wanted and knew how to get it. They were not schoolboys—they were doctors, professors, army officers, and business professionals. They were men and women willing to give up comfort and family and, if necessary, their very lives to bring this country to its senses.

The early tactics hadn't worked? Well then, stronger medicine was in order.

There would be some changes.

Soda dispensers fizzed, upbeat organ music bounced from the walls, and wooden slats rumbled under the rhythmic churn of skates. Whizzing, shrieking, colliding young singles-about a hundred of them-churned in a human whirlpool. Calvary Independent Church's "College and Career Night" at Rocky Springs Roller Rink was a smash. Here, no awkward adolescents shuffled along the edge gripping the rail, pushing up their glasses. No ladies-room debutantes clustered in front of the mirrors for superfluous facial touch-ups. No would-be matchmakers bore spurious messages of secret love.

These were adults. Relaxed. Confident. Socially at ease.

Brenda Gardner, a tall honey-blond college senior, scooted along, wondering if she was ever going to meet some of these guys. Ugh, there she went again, thinking about that. She mustn't do that.

The attractive girl shook her head as if to dispel the thought and rounded a curve. She was certainly not the boy-crazy type. Plenty of other things held her interest—music, studies, her basketball team. And she had scores of friends on campus whom she dearly loved, guys and girls both. Lancaster Bible College was that kind of place.

It was just that she could still remember that summer after her freshman year, down in South America. She had returned to visit her folks at the

Wycliffe Bible Translators center in Colombia. One of the single women working with some Indians near the Venezuelan border needed a tribal partner for three weeks. They couldn't send a man, of course, and Brenda was the only girl around, and . . . .

It hadn't been that bad. In fact, that first taste of tribal work had been rather fulfilling—helping the Cuivas with pre-reading exercises, teaching them to match shapes, and so forth. Actually, that's what had started her seriously considering a linguistics-related career.

But to spend the rest of her life in the jungle with another female translator. . . . She had heard it was like having all the problems of marriage with none of the benefits.

Brenda fought with herself. No, she had settled that issue three weeks ago, around Christmas. If working overseas with some Indian tribe was what God wanted from her, she would do it. Even if it meant being single. So there.

She rounded the rink another time or two.

Still, it would be nice. . . .

Brenda surveyed the skaters. Such a large group. She didn't even know many of them. Of the boys she did know there was a printer, a farmer, a pre-law student. . . . Who would be even remotely interested in linguistics?

She scolded herself. This was silly.

"How ya doin'?"

The voice in her ears made her jerk slightly, and she realized she had been concentrating on the floor. On her right was a boy she had met only with a passing "hi" one Sunday morning in church.

"Hi, Chet."

She hoped she hadn't been muttering to herself.

Chet was the kind of guy who said hi to everybody. Maybe that was part of his job as the college-and-career-group president.

"So what do you think about this big rack-a-boom fun time?" he said with a grin.

"Oh," she began, thinking of how to respond. "It's pretty good I think."

"Fallen yet?"

She smiled and shook her head.

"How long have you been coming to Calvary?"

They dodged a tripped-up skater.

"Oh, pretty much my whole time at Lancaster Bible," she answered.

"That's funny—I grew up in Pennsylvania and went down south for college. You used to live down in South America and came up here for school.

Brenda smiled and nodded. Yes, it was funny. (If his job meant more than just saying hi, who was she to complain?) Yes, she did have a nice Christmas. Yes, she did like her school. Yes, you are rather handsome and have a nice smile and a nice personality and I'd better think of something to say quick before you get bored and skate off.

"What do you do, Chet?" She spoke loudly to be heard above the roar of the skates.

"I work for my dad in a scale business."

"But you graduated from Columbia Bible, didn't you?"

"That's right."

"Do you plan to stay in the scale business or what?"

"Maybe. I feel torn. I was toying with going to North Dakota this June for a course called the Summer Insti—"

"Summer Institute of Linguistics?" Brenda interrupted, nearly halting.

Chet lit up. "You know about it?"

"I went to SIL just last summer in Norman, Oklahoma." Her voice betrayed only a fraction of her excitement.

"No joke? What was it like? 1 may find out it's not for me and save myself a lot of money."

From that point on their meandering conversation shifted into hyper-thrust. Brenda described the courses in detail and Chet confided his struggles over his future.

"My father would like me to work into his scale company. He needs an office manager—he's been feeling the pinch for years. My brother Curt has more mechanical savvy than I do, and it just seems natural to daddy that since I always did better academically Curt would cover the road work and I'd oversee the office."

He told her he didn't know if he had what it took to be a linguist but that he wanted to find out.

"I'm just not sure I can see myself fixing scales for the rest of my life. I'm not even sure I could be a church youth director and spend ninety percent of my time playing basketball with kids and only ten percent having little devotionals with them. You know what I mean?"

"I think so."

"I don't know. I guess somebody's got to do it. But there are a lot more takers for slots like that than there are people out in the boonies translating the Bible for primitive groups."

Brenda could hardly believe her ears.

"I've only got seventy-five years on this earth at best," he said. "I want to use them to give someone the Bible."

When she walked back to her dormitory that evening, Brenda felt as if she were still skating.

Few of the usual romantic trappings characterized Chet's and Brenda's relationship over the next two months. A chance encounter in the aisle after church, an occasional exchange at college and career get-togethers—like swimmers checking the water's temperature with their toes, they eased rather than dived into each others lives.

But as the weeks went by, the chance encounters became less chance and more encounter. Chet and Brenda still didn't act like a dating couple—they never kept to themselves in the presence of others. Nor did they play romantic cat and mouse. From the beginning they realized that, as a man and woman who enjoyed each other's company, their paths would eventually merge or separate. Brenda was committed to linguistics, Chet was unsure. But the freedom to openly discuss such things relaxed them both. Chet confided that he would never again kiss a girl he did not intend to marry. Brenda understood. By their first date in April they were like old friends.

At the end of the summer Brenda's parents came up from Colombia for her college graduation. The Bittermans invited the Gardners for dinner and afterwards Chet found himself downstairs in the shop working on a scale with Mr. Gardner.

"I understand you and your father work on some pretty heavy equipment."

"Sometimes," answered Chet, tinkering with adjustments. "We get everything from big mamas on down to little scofers like this one. Could you hand me that rag, please, Mr. Gardner?"

"George."

"Thanks, George." Chet took the cloth. Most of the missionaries Chet had met over the years were linguists or Bible teachers. Brenda's father was a support worker. "You said you were a financial advisor or something down in Colombia?"

"An accountant. I oversee the finance office at our outpost center, Lomalinda."

"Lomalinda . . . sounds exotic."

"It is, in some ways. It means 'pretty hill.' Lomalinda's in the sub-tropics, pretty far from most everything. It's made up of grassy knolls. Dirt roads wind over and around them, connecting the buildings.

The two men knelt over the scale as Chet worked.

"Are we talking thatched roofs or what?"

"No—inexpensive American-style homes. Practical. Low maintenance. There's a central generator so we have electric lights, indoor plumbing, and so forth."

"Not bad for a life of sacrifice."

"It's a little tougher out in the tribes, Chet. Most everybody lives in thatch huts out there. And getting there . . . well, I'm thinking of one family. To reach their mountain tribe they take one of our own planes to Bogota, the capital city. Next day they catch a commercial flight to another city, then they have an eight-hour bus trip on some difficult roads to a little hole-in-the-wall town at the foot of some mountains."

"Quite a jaunt," said Chet.

"And they're still not there. Now they begin a two-day hike up and down mountain trails that would challenge a pack mule."

The adventurer in Chet stirred.

"Why Lomalinda, then?"

"A center of operations, a kind of headquarters. Parents couldn't keep their children out in the tribe year round. And they themselves need breaks from the isolation. Then, too, with boiling drinking water, treating medical problems, gathering firewood— there just isn't that much time out in the tribe to analyze the data they collect. So, they return to Lomalinda and plug into the twentieth century, so to speak, which allows them time to analyze their data and discuss the language with consultants.

"And that's where you worked?"

"Yes," nodded George. "Brenda loved growing up there."

Chet said he could understand why. She had told him how high school kids used to go alligator hunting on dates, and how some of them had monkeys and boas for pets.

"But you didn't move down there till she was in ninth grade, did you? What'd you do before that?"

George sat on a crate. "I worked for Texaco in their Maryland accounting office."

Chet straightened up.

"Can I ask you a personal question?"

"Sure."

"When you had a regular job . . . what made you leave?"

"Well . . . ."

"I mean, how'd you know you were supposed to?"

"You mean 'know' as in some dream or . . . ."

"No, no. I assume you didn't get that. But there's nothing wrong with working for Texaco. How did you decide God wanted you overseas?"

Mr. Gardner thought. "How old were you in 1956?"

"Four."

"Then you probably don't recall it firsthand. But maybe you heard about the five American missionaries who were speared to death in Ecuador trying to make contact with a primitive tribe."

Chet nodded.

"*Life* magazine ran a photo series of the aftermath. They showed the beach, the bodies—everything." He started talking with his hands. "Up till then Joan and I didn't realize that there were still people in remote parts of the world who had never heard about a God who loved them."

Chet nodded his head. "I remember the story."

"The incident really stirred us. As the years went by Joan and I became more and more concerned about such tribes. Often when we read the Bible or heard a sermon we thought about the Indians those missionaries gave their lives to help. I thought about the comfortable office I was sitting in. Somehow, it didn't add up. We struggled inside, hoping the thoughts would go away. We loved our job and home and wanted to be content. But we weren't. We knew God was speaking to us."

George got up and stretched his legs. "In looking at various mission organizations we found there was a need not only for preachers and Bible translators but for people with other skills—plumbers, mechanics, computer men—"

" Accountants, " Chet interrupted.

"That's right."

"But how did you know that you were supposed to go?"

"Chet, I suppose we just stopped asking ourselves 'Why go?' and started asking ourselves 'Why not?' There was a need, we had the skills to match, and God had made us willing."

"Didn't you come up with any negatives?"

"Sure. We didn't want to leave our home, our friends, our country. But we knew God wanted us to. That overrode everything. A man can stand just about anything if he knows he's where God wants him."

"And here you are," said Chet.

"And here I am," said George, smiling.

"And here I am," said Chet, closing his tool box. "I'm not sure why."

One week later, Brenda watched her hitchhiking sweetheart disappear down the horizon. She returned to her apartment, her heart on the road with him to the Summer Institute of Linguistics in North Dakota. A plain white envelope on the kitchen table bearing her name in familiar handwriting snatched her breath. Grabbing a butterknife she carefully slid it under the flap.

It was a Soft Touch card.

Mr. Bitterman spent that summer in his basement office, wanting a manager, frequently recalling his 1952 promise to God that the baby in Mary's arms was His to do with as He wished.

Brenda spent the summer in a car with her family visiting the churches that supported their overseas work—giving reports, renewing ties, hoping for long-distance calls.

Chet spent the summer in the pits, drowning in a

world of grammar and phonology. He entered, not knowing a morpheme from a head of lettuce. Within two weeks he wasn't even sure about the lettuce. The enormity of the workload competed with the inscrutability of the material. By day, phonemics, phonetics, and phonology barraged his intellect. By night a loneliness for Brenda ached in his chest. When he fell asleep, late in the evening, a cacophony of labials, fricatives, and glottalized stops rang in his ears.

His letters to Brenda (always saturated with Bible verses) grew longer and more intense. An early July letter included the following:

> On Thursday I was about ready to quit. I was completely lost in grammar class and about 3/4 lost in phonology, and you know how phonetics goes. I mean, it just seemed like God had answered all my prayers and shown me He did not want me in translation work. . . . It seems like this stuff is for A people and I'm a Z person. I was tired of bending myself to fit something I wasn't.
>
> Right now it probably looks like I'll end up working for my dad. Some days I think one thing and some days the other. But I can honestly say that I am completely neutral in the face of His will. I do not in any way feel that mission work is more exalted than scale work. The only thing that places a higher value on one as opposed to another is what God wants me to do. . . .
>
> I've thought about the ramifications this has on us. . . . I know that should God lead me back home into scales, I cannot think of you in terms of any long range commitment.

Several things kept Chet going during those despairing months. First, there were Brenda's letters, affectionate and intensely personal, filling a spot inside that had always lain empty. Then, there was a lunchroom conversation one day with a linguistics professor and his wife. Both of them were graduates of Columbia Bible College and the woman's father happened to be Cameron Townsend, the founder of Wycliffe Bible Translators.

"Chet," she said, "I've often heard my dad say that the ones who make the best translators are the ones who really have to plug away at it, not the ones who get it all with a snap."

"Why is that?"

"Because when you get to another culture it takes a lot of stick-with-it to become accepted by the people and transcribe their language. If you're accustomed to everything quick and easy, you probably won't last. But the person who has to work hard at linguistics won't be surprised to find he has to work hard out in the bush."

Chet's third shot in the arm, the one that finally saw him through, came during August finals. "Dear, Dear Brenda," he wrote, describing it,

> Monday I really felt like it was impossible to study—I just couldn't get into it. It seemed like so much stuff, a lot of which I didn't really know. So after supper I went up to my room and talked with God for a while. I told God how tired I was and how much I didn't want to study, how much I didn't know, etc. I told Him that if I got a B or better on this test, not a B-, I would know for sure that He wanted me to pursue Wycliffe further. There was a chance I could get a C or perhaps even a C+; but I knew there was almost no chance I'd get a B-, and, that a B was out of the question. . . . Brenda, I just knew I wasn't prepared, and worse than that, I didn't feel like studying at all.

The exam was 9 pages long. We started at 8:40 and had to hand them in at 12:00. The first two or three pages had relatively easy problems on them, but the farther you got the harder they got. At 11:00 I hadn't started the last 2 pages yet. On page 8 I got really frustrated because I could remember having studied the very thing they were asking, but I couldn't quite put it together. (I studied until 3:00 A.M.) I finally slopped down the essentials for the last 2 pages and handed it in at 12:00. I went back up to my room, and I really felt bad about it. I prayed again and just gave it all to Him again: the test, my grammar grade, Wycliffe, you, etc. I was scared to see my grade.

Today when I went to my mailbox, I got your letter and my test back. I got a B on my grammar test. Brenda, I just felt so grateful to God! I was so happy! Brenda, I know you had to be praying for me! Then I got your letter and opened it up and read it. It was so full of your love and warmth; it was just like you! . . . . I felt overwhelmed with a sense of God's love and intervention in my life. I just know He loves me. It seems like, sometimes, you go a long time with a dry spell, and then, God shows you all at once all over again. So that's why I feel especially close to you tonight, as well as close to God.

At summer's end Chet packed his bags, stuck out his thumb, and headed east. Brenda passed the time by filling out an application for membership with Wycliffe. "I believe," she included on her doctrinal statement, "that the bodies of the just will be raised." The morning of August 19, she answered a knock on her door and for twenty-four intoxicating hours the young friends drank in each other's company. But by lunch the next day Chet had mounted his cycle for Pennsylvania and Brenda was packing for Dallas and a second dose of her own linguistics training.

A flurry of letters passed between Dallas and Lancaster that fall. Then at Christmas time, pen and ink gave way to face to face in Maryland. Twinkling tree lights were the couple's only company that first evening together. They sat up late on Grandmom Gardner's sofa—sharing, listening, enjoying the quiet.

"I've got a question to ask you." Chet had turned his head from the soft colors and was staring at Brenda. He leaned over and kissed her.

"Well?"

Brenda met his gaze and returned his smile.

"Sure, Chet." They grinned from ear to ear. Whatever lay ahead, they were in it together.

Another Group, Another Movement

What did lie ahead? Membership in an organization with an ambitious agenda and unusual origins.

1917, Guatemala, Central America

Fresh off a steamship from Los Angeles, twenty-one-year-old William Cameron Townsend got down to the work he had come to do: to share his faith and distribute Spanish Bibles. He approached a pedestrian and inquired in halting Spanish, "Do you know the Lord Jesus?" Taking the word "Señor" to mean "Mr." instead of "Lord," and "Jesus" to be the common first name that it was, the man replied, "No. I'm new here myself. Sorry."

Sobered but undeterred, young Townsend procured a pack mule and began a circuit through Central America's highlands among the once-proud Cakchiquel Indians. He spent the next two years learning that Spanish was a foreign language to most of them. His Bibles were worthless.

"If your God is so great, why doesn't he speak our language?" a bilingual Cakchiquel asked him one day. The question stirred Townsend to the quick. Without benefit of linguistics training or even a college degree, he set out to address the objection. Eleven years later the Cakchiquels saw the first copy of the New Testament in their own tongue. God *did* speak their language, a language so complex that a single verb could have as many as 100,000 different forms. Cameron Townsend had accomplished the incredible—likened by one linguist to "learning brain surgery with no formal training"—and in the process had founded five Indian schools, an orphanage, a printing press, a clinic, and a coffee cooperative.

Jesus was no longer Spanish. He was Cakchiquel.

At that time the science of linguistics was still in its infancy, and the unwritten languages of the world were believed to number about six hundred. "One down, five hundred and ninety-nine to go" was Cam Townsend's attitude.

Wycliffe Bible Translators had been born.

* * *

1964. The Jungles of Colombia, South America

Hunched over a card table that crowded his long legs, Al Wheeler sat on a bench in his hut on the Putumayo River, studying the page before him by the light of a single candle. His alma mater, the University of California, was preparing its hundredth anniversary report by making a survey of selected graduates. Having begun work toward his Ph.D. in linguistics at the university, he had spent the last four years among the Siona Indians with his wife, Peggy, plugging away at one of the two-thousand known, unwritten languages of the world.

Indicate your total yearly income, the questionnaire read.

Al circled the smallest figure on the form.

How many automobiles do you own?

Zero. None were needed in the jungle.

How many homes do you own?

He glanced around at the split palm floor, thatched roof, and bamboo walls. "One," he started to write. Then he considered the passage in St. John where Jesus talks of the home awaiting believers in heaven. After a moment he put down "Two."

Do you own a boat?

"Yes," he checked. Space did not allow a description of the dugout canoe on the river bank.

Do you plan to travel abroad for vacation purposes next year?

His family's furlough was coming up next April, and certainly some of their time at home would be spent vacationing. "Yes."

Do you rent quarters elsewhere?

"Yes." Periodically he had business in Bogota where, for $1.09 a night, he could rent a room at Wycliffe's guest house.

The linguist grinned with satisfaction at his replies. Nobody could look down his nose at a prestigious job like this. No sir. Wycliffe Bible Translators was liable to attract promising young couples from all over.

August 4, 1976. The Neighborhood of La Soledad, Bogota, Colombia

About midnight, two sedans rounded a corner and eased their way between cars parked on both sides of the narrow, unlit street. The drivers parked and made their way up the sidewalk toward an apartment building door. One of them fumbled for the key as their families sleepily disembarked from the vehicles.

So this is the guest house, thought Will Kindberg.

Nothing distinguished it from the other Spanish-style row homes, several stories high, that flanked the street. It felt good to be out and stretching after the tiring trip from Peru. It would feel even better to get unpacked and settled into this new position with Wycliffe.

A small parcel in the shadows on the step caught his attention.

"Oh look," he chuckled, "somebody's left us a bomb."

As his companion toyed with the lock, Will stooped to pick up the package. A tiny electrical component on top began sparkling.

"It *is* a bomb!" his friend shouted. The man dropped the key and raced to the car for shelter.

Will froze. Should he throw it in the street? His family and friends were there. Leave it on the steps? People were inside; but at least a door protected them.

Gently he set the package down then, sprinted behind the car and crouched, wondering what it would feel like to have his feet blown off.

The explosion ripped the night. Will buried his face in his hands and listened as bits of glass rained on the pavement up and down the street. "Welcome to Colombia," he muttered, ears ringing from the concussion.

Somebody didn't like Wycliffe.

* * *

April 1978, Miami International Airport

Avianca Flight #007, Miami to Bogota, taxied to the runway. The plane was filled to capacity with chattering passengers all but oblivious to the flight attendant's safety speech.

A middle-aged man in a green leisure suit stared out the window from seat 27A. Beside him, his wife flipped through the airline magazine, her mind not on her reading. Sitting next to the woman in the aisle seat was Wycliffe administrator Bernie May, a friendly faced executive dressed in a gray suit and topped with a crew cut.

"Hi. I'm sardine 27C."

The couple returned Bernie's smile. "It is a bit crowded in here."

"Bernie May." The Wycliffe executive extended his hand.

"Roy Dickers. My wife, Alice."

"First time out of the U.S.?" asked Bernie.

"Yes," the husband and wife answered simultaneously, then looked at each other and laughed. "You could never guess we're excited, could you?"

Bernie chuckled. "I think you'll enjoy Latin America."

"You've been before?" asked Alice.

"I lived there fifteen years. Two of my children were born in Peru."

"Fifteen years," exclaimed Roy. "What sort of taste did it leave in your mouth?"

The jet shot down the runway. "Banana," he said with a grin as the aircraft drowned out his voice.

Once the plane had burst through the cloud cover and Miami was no longer in sight, Roy and Alice turned from the window and posed questions to Bernie about the "other" America.

Alice was concerned over stories about high crime rates in the larger cities. Bernie responded by asking if the situation was any different in Manhattan or Los· Angeles.

"Tell me about business," said Roy. "I hear things are slow there. Can't get parts, can't get service, items back-ordered for weeks."

"I know what you're saying. But there are reasons for that in Latin countries."

"Such as?"

"Well, the heat, for instance. Outside the mountains it gets incredibly hot. Ten-thirty in the morning and it's sweltering. You just can't keep a cold-climate pace. Then, too, for these people time and production aren't as important as relationships.

If a Latin has an eleven o'clock appointment and meets a friend on the sidewalk at ten fifty-five, he's not going to say, 'Hey listen, I'd love to hear about your father in the hospital but I've really got to go.'"

"And the fellow waiting behind the desk at eleven o'clock isn't upset?"

"Why should he be?" laughed Bernie. "He's probably not there himself!"

Roy shook his head. "How can they afford to operate like that?"

"They can't afford not to. They need each other more than we do—or, at least than we think we do."

As an example, Bernie noted the inconvenience and uncertainty caused by political instability in many Latin nations. Accustomed to such vagaries, citizens tended to stick together and pool resources.

"Latins are tremendously creative people. They're geniuses at doing without. I've seen a man make a drive shaft for his car out of a broom stick because he couldn't locate a bona fide replacement. It's a tremendous thing to see. I love those people.

The couple nodded.

"You said you lived in Peru for fifteen years," said Alice. "What did you do there?"

"I flew planes for an organization called Wycliffe Bible Translators."

The name, he explained, came from John Wycliffe, a fourteenth-century scholar who had first translated the Bible into English. The organization's task was to develop alphabets for Indian tribes whose languages had never been written. It would then teach tribesmen to read and, finally, would translate the Bible and books on health and agriculture into the local tongue.

"Then we work with them in bilingual education—which helps incorporate them into the national life of their country." '

"It sounds challenging, Mr. May," said Alice.

Bernie smiled. "More so all the time."

Roy wrinkled his brow. "How so?"

Bernie sighed. "Since 1975 it's been an increasing challenge to keep on good terms with the governments that host us. That was the year President Ford off-handedly remarked at a press conference that the C.I.A. sometimes uses missionaries as agents."

"That's disgusting," clucked Alice. She looked at Bernie. "Well, do they?"

Bernie held up both palms. "You're asking the wrong man! If so, they certainly don't use us.'

Everyone in SIL knows he'll be immediately dismissed if he's ever caught running errands for Intelligence. "

"SIL?" said Roy.

"Sorry. Summer Institute of Linguistics. That's what we're known as overseas. The name grew out of our training course."

Roy wagged his head. "So one presidential slip of the tongue and suddenly every foreigner carrying a Bible has a dagger beneath his trench coat, eh?"

"Actually, the problem started even before that," answered Bernie. "'We've taken a beating in the overseas press for almost a decade. I get newspaper clippings about SIL sent to me every day from around the world. You should see them. One day an editorial claims we're a U.S. government front. (Mentioning the U.S. is always good for effect.) The next day we're shipping home uranium for Uncle Sam to manufacture bombs, or cooperating with multi-national corporations. Or, and this is the big one, contributing to the economic and cultural exploitation of the indigenous population."

"What's that?" Alice's words mirrored Roy's expression.

"Big-brothering the Indians. Shoving religion on them. Changing their culture."

"Who puts the stuff in the papers?"

"Ah!" Bernie held up a finger. "Let me tell you something interesting. An editorial from professor so-and-so at such-and-such university will appear one day in Lima, Peru, attacking SIL's work among the Indians. Lo and behold, the next day translations popup in papers in Bogota, Cairo, Nairobi, and Sydney. What's that tell you?

"Or Radio Havana broadcasts a harangue about SIL's crimes of ethnocide and capitalist oppression against primitive minority groups and a leftist French news service shoots it worldwide in no time."

"Are you saying Communists are behind this?" asked Alice.

Bernie wrinkled his face in only partial agreement. "Alice, I'm not saying there's a back room in the Kremlin where someone sits orchestrating this media blitz. But radical Marxism has so permeated the social sciences in Latin America that when you meet an anthropologist or political scientist, chances are the party's manifesto isn't collecting any dust on his shelf. And it's not just the academic world. There's a sizable knot of religious zealots down there who are convinced that the kingdom of God is right here and now, and that the only way to usher it in is with bullets and grenades. Class struggle, throwing off oppressors—that's the work of God."

"And these social scientists and so-called religious people are the ones writing the articles?" said Roy.

"They're the ones who sign the press releases."

"And readers take them seriously?"

Bernie explained just how seriously. In early 1975 the Colombian branch director was driving his jeep across SIL's center in the sub-tropics when a twin turbine military helicopter suddenly appeared over a hill and set down. Simultaneously two transport trucks pulled up loaded with soldiers and frogmen. Several generals and other high-ranking officials disembarked from the copter, produced their field orders, and stated their intention to search the grounds.

"Search for what?" asked Roy.

"Missiles, uranium, spy equipment, you name it."

Roy laughed.

"No kidding," said Bernie. "They asked to see the authorizations for our planes and radios and asked why we had a fence around the property and why the airstrip was so short."

"And you said?"

"We told them the fence was to keep out stray cattle and discourage robbers. It was only a few feet high. We showed them our papers and explained that because our planes are used mainly for jungle flights, they're equipped to take off and land in tight places; we didn't need a longer airstrip. The military was concerned we might be deliberately trying to keep out other type aircraft."

"Well," asked Alice, "were they satisfied?"

"Yes, once they checked everything. They searched it all—language files, planes, radio equipment. They even had the frogmen comb the lake bottom. Once we got over the initial shock we were glad to have them come so they could put the rumors to bed."

"Did they really believe the rumors?" asked Alice.

"The government?" answered Bernie. "I don't think so. But with all that had been in the papers they needed to investigate and make a statement."

"I'd be interested in what you answered about big-brothering the Indians," said Roy.

"The military really didn't go into that."

"Supposing they had. What would you say?"

"About changing their culture? Well, I guess if you consider how the death rate drops after Indians learn simple hygiene, how literacy fosters learning, how intertribal warfare all but stops when they embrace the teachings of Christ, and how they no longer live in terror of spirits because they believe in a God who loves them—yeah, I'd say we've had some impact on the culture."

Roy nodded. The man's point made sense. His group had helped the Indians. Still, in the long run, wasn't it best just to leave folks alone to work out their own lives? *National Geographic* photos of remote jungle peoples wearing Levis and chewing Bazooka bubble gum came to his mind. It didn't seem natural. He shared his thoughts aloud.

"Roy," Bernie said, setting down his orange juice, "civilization, or whatever you want to call it, is creeping into the jungle faster than you would believe. I've seen soda cans flowing down rivers sixty miles from the nearest town. Goodness, the lion's share of folks out there aren't even missionaries! They're businessmen trying to sell transistor radios or chain saws or whatever else they can dump. Or they're drug middlemen paying Indians to raise coke instead of manioc so they can turn it over in Miami at a thousand percent profit! The question isn't if outsiders are going to come. It's who. Who's going to get there first—people who love Indians and teach them to read and cope with the twentieth century, or people who'll milk them for everything they've got, then discard them like disposable bottles?"

Bernie's eyes held Roy's and Alice's for several seconds.

"You people are dead serious about your work, aren't you?" said Roy.

Bernie nodded. "'Dead serious.'"

"You must hate the people who try to stop you."

"Hate them?" Bernie asked. "I feel sorry for them. I get frustrated with them. But hate them?" He shook his head. "What good does it do to love an Indian if you hate a Communist?"

* * *

July 1978. The Mountainous Jungles of Extreme Southern Mexico

He knew that something unexpected might happen, and he hardly dared to hope that they would pass without fearful adventure over these great tall mountains with lonely peaks and valleys where no king ruled. . . .

. . . They were high up in a narrow place, with a dreadful fall into a dim valley at one side of them. There they were sheltering under a hanging rock for the night, and he lay beneath a blanket and shook from head to toe. [1]

The distant campfires had all died, each in its turn, as the evening had deepened. But one fire crackled on, seeming to enjoy the adventures of *The Hobbit* as much as Brenda Bitterman who sat on a stump beside her husband as he read aloud. The slope of their mountainside outpost was steep—one wouldn't want to fall off the wrong side of the hammock. Others had set up camp on gentler ground, farther from the rapids, but Chet had chosen this spot for its isolation and beauty.

The young mother listened to the night sounds, trying to absorb the jungle's presence with all of her senses. She loved these times alone with Chet, after dark when the baby was asleep. During the day they were too busy with meal preparation and classes on wilderness techniques to enjoy the time together.

"In my hand is cheeb," the lecturer said their first day. "A more tasteless, nutritionless plant you'll never find. But chew on the heart and it will stay your hunger pangs."

---

[1] J.R.R. Tolkien, *The Hobbit* (Boston: Houghton Mifflin Co., 1956), pp. 66, 68.

Rope hammocks, herbal medicine, compass reading—hopefully some of it would come to mind if they ever found themselves surviving a forest plane crash.

The Wycliffe training experience called Jungle Camp was half over. Seven weeks down, seven to go. What one didn't have to go through to get into Wycliffe! She scratched at a mosquito bite and stared about. The little set-up of hammocks, makeshift stick table, and vine-rope playpen had been home over the past few days.

Home. Brenda wondered how long it would be before they could call some place "home" and mean it. Linguistic courses in North Dakota, church meetings in Maryland, cross-cultural studies in Texas, and now, Mexico. They hadn't stopped running since the day they were married.

"I want to be a hard-working type person that stays so busy he has no time for petty things," Chet had once said. He wasn't kidding. Wycliffe wasn't kidding either, thought Brenda as she sipped tea from a tin cup, straining the leaves with her teeth. Thatched huts, twenty-five mile hikes, pre-dawn work assignments. She smiled at those first seven weeks being called Main Base. It sounded too civilized. No doubt those fifty days were the most stressful the majority of them had ever encountered.

Yet Main Base was only the beginning, the first and most comfortable of a series of experiences designed to weed out the ill-suited and equip the determined. Soon, each family would be assigned to a separate Indian village to make do on their own for six weeks. One day—one never knew when—a staff member would appear and give the word

You're on for survival hike tomorrow. Be at Main Base at 6:00 A.M."

No one knew beforehand precisely what awaited him in this last phase of training. Returnees from previous expeditions were not allowed to say. All a trainee knew was that he would be hiked a great distance up steep mountain gorges, dropped off by himself, and expected to stay put until a staff member came for him—quelling his hunger and combating the elements as best he knew how.

Brenda would be excused from survival hike because of her baby. She wasn't sure which would be harder—tramping through dense jungle with an empty stomach or staying alone back in the Indian village with her husband gone. As for Chet—he would have no problems. On mountain treks he often carried the packs of others who had less stamina.

A moth flickered into the campsite, cozying up to the rays of the dying fire. Brenda tossed out her tea leaves and gazed at Chet who sat studying the embers. Soon they'd be farther south, in Costa Rica, living with a Spanish–speaking family, studying the language. A few days' respite in the States and then they'd leave for good. For Colombia. Would it have changed? Would it be the same Colombia she had known as a high-school girl?

She didn't know. And in one sense, she didn't care. They would spend their lives in Colombia. Their place was with the Indians.

Detours

One year later, August 1979, found the Bittermans at the Wycliffe outpost center in Colombia— closer to, but not yet with, an Indian tribe.

From his vantage point in the radio tower Chet watched as a flock of parrots swooped over the lake. In the trees below them, howler monkeys shouted frenzied greetings to the rising Colombian sun. He scanned the green hills and valleys of Lomalinda, watching motorbikes weave their patterns of dust all over the mile-square center. The homes, post office, grocery store, and other buildings sat clearly in view. Beside him a half-read copy of *Treasure Island* lay on a folding chair where it would remain all morning. Radio traffic was brisk. It was tribal check-in time.

"Los Angeles. Lomalinda." He spoke into the microphone, calling a cluster of jungle huts two hours' flight east. Janet Barnes, a blond-haired translator from California, worked there among the Tuyuca Indians.

"Lomalinda. Los Angeles." All radio communications were in Spanish allowing anyone who wished to monitor them.

"Good morning, Los Angeles. How are you today? Over."

"Good morning, Lomalinda. We're fine. We have a message to pass—a grocery order to be sent out on the next flight. We can wait till you've finished with your other traffic. Over."

"Roger. Roger." Chet replied. "I'll call when I'm free. Lomalinda. Q.A.P."

"OK. Q.A.P."

Chet logged the check-in report. Neat girl, he thought. The Tuyucas loved her. Good storyteller, too. She had once related a confusing conversation between her language partner and an Indian. In Tuyuca, pitch and voice intonation affect a word's meaning. The two linguists had learned that "di" (falling pitch) meant "blood." Janet's partner, whose questions usually ended with an English intonation in which the last word rose, asked the Indian, "Now the word for 'blood' is 'di'?" (Rising pitch).

"No, that means clay."

"Oh," she answered. "What was 'blood'?"

"Di." (Falling pitch)

"Oh, di?" (Rising pitch)

"No, di." (Falling pitch)

Chet grinned, scanning the tribal roster for his next call.

"Cobaria. Lomalinda." He was calling Paul Headland, a resolute translator in his forties who, with his wife, worked among one of Colombia's mountain tribes.

"Lomalinda. Cobaria."

"Good morning."

"How do you copy us? Our battery is a bit low."

"Loud and clear," answered Chet. "I have a message from Bogota. It says, 'Guesthouse reservations confirmed for the fourteenth through the twen—'"

Another frequency interrupted. It was the pilot

of the single engine Helio that Chet could see on
the field below, next to the hangar.

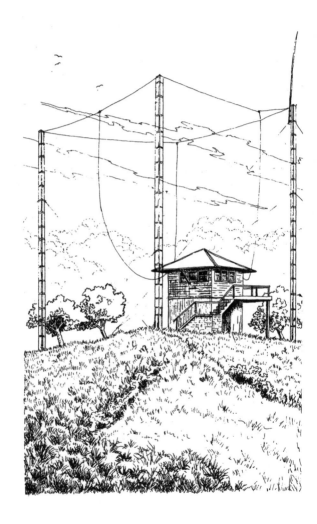

"Lomalinda. Lomalinda. 612."

"Cobaria. Stand by." Chet lifted a lever to change frequencies. "612. Lomalinda. Go ahead."

"612 ready to taxi. Lomalinda to Macuare. Three passengers. Over."

Chet acknowledged the message.

"Roger. Roger."

The plane taxied toward the airstrip and Chet resumed his conversation with the Headlands. As long as he could not yet be in a tribe he was glad to be working the tower. These first two weeks in the job had improved his Spanish immensely. Things would be busy today—some calls from Bogota, checkpoint reports from three outbound planes, and the arrival of several scheduled patches. All planes en route checked in at pre-arranged intervals so the center could pinpoint any that went down. The weather was clear so he would be giving no cloud cover reports.

Chet tried to picture the linguists he spoke with. Paul and Edna Headland worked with the Tunebo Indians, a tribe that considered all people and articles from the outside world contaminated. Their list of taboos was endless—no eating an outsider's food, or receiving his gifts, or using his matches. Visitors were asked to sit on banana leaves that got discarded after a visit.

"They won't teach you the language," a nearby settler warned the Headlands. "They'll point to a dog and call it a shoe. They'll point to a tree and call it the sky, till you're so confused you give up. "

A Spanish-speaking Tunebo had fulfilled the prophecy by providing a host of false vocabulary.

The most frustrating taboo was against paper. Anything written upon it possessed a power beyond man's understanding or manipulation. The prohibition forced any Tunebo interested in the translators' books to abandon home for the outside world, a price few were willing to pay.

"Lomalinda. 612."

"612. Go ahead."

The pilot was ready for takeoff. Chet monitored the departure.

"612 departed from Lomalinda at 1210, climbing to 5.5, estimating Candelejas at 25, and final on to Macuare at 1305. Over."

Chet acknowledged his reception. "612 leaving Lomalinda at 1210, Candelejas 25, Macuare 1305. Over."

"You got it. 612. Q.A.P."

"Q.A.P."

The Spanish flowed like water; that felt good. Chet watched the Helio circle into its pattern, thinking how the linguists must welcome the sight of it. He wondered if the Henriksen family resented their mountain region's inability to receive a plane. The closest strip to them was a two-day's hike over steep terrain, followed by an eight-hour bus ride. For almost two years they had bent their backs to the task of clearing trees for a strip of their own—leveling dirt and shoring up a foundation with palm wood strips. Finally the test day came. A Helio touched down, skidded off the perpetually soaked earth, and crashed into the bank, bending part of the wing.

Something about a challenging situation like that appealed to Chet. He wasn't sure why. Perhaps it was the contrast with what he'd been doing since he and Brenda arrived in May.

"Chet, you have a way with people," the

personnel director told him. "We'd like you to organize recreation for the language helpers." So, Friday nights he had set up games for the Indians that linguists frequently brought back to the center.

"Chet, we'd like you to do some paperwork for a few weeks."

"Chet, we need a man in the radio tower." He and Brenda had known before they came that the shortage of support workers forced every linguist into a service job for several months. He could accept that—God had put them under certain authorities and God didn't make mistakes. Besides, apart from his longing to decide on a tribe and get to work, he enjoyed life at Lomalinda. Where else did an entire congregation come to church on motorcycles—two, three, sometimes four to a bike? True, their temporary quarters were cramped, but they hoped to buy their own house soon.

Chet had enjoyed his hours at the Technical Studies Department the past summer. Every day he would park his Honda in front of the cinder block building and make his way to a sparsely furnished back office with no windows. There he would remain till lunch, fingering through files on the fifteen known tribes in the country still without a written language. The more a tribe had come into contact with outsiders, the more was known about it and the thicker its file was.

Chet spent most of his time in the thinner files.

Chami. An interesting name. Population approximately three thousand. Mostly agrarian. Some domesticated animals. Wet climate. Mountainous.

Retuama. Hmm. A jungle group in the state of Amazonas. River people. Large pavilion-type huts.

Dietary mainstay: fish, wild pig, manioc. He glanced in the folders of several other jungle tribes. Manioc. Manioc. That's what everyone planted. He understood it wasn't all they planted.

Carijonas.

Yukpas.

Agualinda. Guahibos.

Each had a fascination of its own. But he felt drawn to the jungle areas more than the mountains or plains. Kipling's *Jungle Book* had stirred Chet as a boy, and the flame of wonder was still lit.

As he flipped through the photos, descriptions, and survey reports from military expeditions and anthropological teams, one tribe repeatedly caught his attention. "This group lives in southern Colombia close to the Brazilian border," the report read.

> No outsider has been able to establish friendly, permanent relations with them. They are well-built, ranging from 5' 0" to 5' 8". Outsiders call them Carabayo, after a courageous fighter of local folklore. Carabayo bodies are beautifully decorated in intricate designs with dark paint. Wooden ear plugs fill an inch-wide ear hole, and the men wear two bands around their upper arm, one above and one below the biceps. The men wear a G-string while the women wear a short, wraparound skirt. The exact size of this language group has not been determined. . . . The strategy for contacting the Carabayos would have to be worked out carefully. . . .

The tower phone rang. It was Brenda. Yes, he could stop by Lackey's on his way home for lunch and bring Anna Ruth.

He knew he had an exceptional wife. Eight months pregnant and still she kept herself and the house looking nice—always a smile and some wild flowers in a vase when her husband walked in.

Interestingly, she, too, had come under the spell of the Carabayos, independently of Chet. When she and Chet compared notes for the first time, they knew they were on to something. The situation had looked good for the family to attempt an initial contact in the late summer. But then they learned of an expedition planned by French anthropologists for the end of September. The government would never grant two groups permission to enter so closely together. He hoped that somehow things would work out for him and Brenda to enter.

Morning passed quickly in the sweltering radio tower. Reception was clear and the flights checked in without incident. It was a minute or two after 612 reached its jungle town destination that the pilot's voice crackled over the monitor.

"Lomalinda. 612."

"612. Lomalinda. Go ahead." There was something strange in George DeVoucalla's tone.

"I'm sitting on the strip—have not unboarded yet. Two armed men are approaching the plane. I can't read the situation but it doesn't look good. Keep your ears glued. If I don't call in within ten minutes, I'm in trouble."

Chet's brow wrinkled. He had better notify the support affairs director. His mind flashed back to 1978, before he and Brenda had arrived, when one of the single women in a jungle tribe had made such a call. It was 9:00 A.M. Some men were approaching on foot from the far end of her airstrip. Lomalinda requested her to call back every hour that day. When the 10:00 call did not come a plane rushed to her location. The pilot spotted the woman in a boat five miles up river. The terrorists had threatened to kill her if she ever came back. Had she been a man, they said, they would have killed her right then.

Chet shook his head. Violence had threatened more than once. Just this summer the Keels had been at their tribal airstrip loading a plane to return to Lomalinda when five slovenly dressed men rushed out from the jungle and leveled machine guns at them. The barefoot gunmen fired questions and orders in staccato succession. Open the house! Unload the plane! Where are you going?

"Who are you?" the Keels asked.

"Police. Show us your radio permission." Jack Keels produced the folded paper.

"But this is for the State of Meta," the leader snarled.

"We're in Meta," the linguist answered. His inquisitor reddened.

The gunmen ordered the plane unloaded. One of them opened a box and found only empty jars.

"What was in these?"

"Peanut butter," answered Carol. "I can't eat beans because I'm allergic, so I eat a lot of. . . ."

"And in these?"

"Peanut butter."

The men pointed to a third box. "Peanut butter, too?"

Carol nodded.

A white powder scattered on the ground beneath the house's supporting poles caught their attention.

One man reached down and rubbed some granules between his thumb and fingers.

"What is it?"

"Insecticide," Jack answered, not to the man's satisfaction.

The makeshift soldier began sniffing it. "Truthfully, Señor!"

"Powder to kill bugs."

The gunman smiled, still rubbing the powder. He sprinkled a pinch on his tongue. "Tell me, Señora," he grinned at Carol. "What is this powder?"

"My husband told you," she replied irritably in a voice that said: You are stupid. "It's poison."

Suddenly the fact registered and the guerrilla spewed the substance out, coughing and screaming for water. Eyeing his weapon, the Keels fell over themselves obliging him.

After several more gruff orders the gunmen told the Keels they could go and disappeared into the brush as quickly as they had come.

Nestled in his radio tower, overlooking the quiet routine of a Lomalinda day, Chet squinted his eyes in prayer.

"Give George quickness of mind, Lord. Give him courage. Make those men be reasonable. Don't let them act rashly. Don't let them—"

"361. Lomalinda."

Chet grabbed the microphone.

"Lomalinda. "

"It's all right. They were police. They were wondering who I was."

Chet closed his eyes, this time in relief. Thank you, God. They had to keep cool. They mustn't overreact. They could easily take this guerrilla thing too seriously.

* * *

Jeff Smothermon reached for a handkerchief to blot a sweat droplet that had fallen on his notebook before him on the desk. A trail of ink swirled in the tiny puddle. The linguist marveled. To think that these chicken scratches on the loose-leaf before him would one day be in print. To think that the Indians he and Jo had come to love over the past six years would someday find meaning in these strange symbols. Someday they would read for themselves the words of Jesus—in their own tongue—and through those words know their Maker.

He shivered a moment despite the heat.

Outside a cycle motored up and sputtered off. His wife, Jo, entered the backyard office shed, wearing shorts and sandals like her husband.

"Hi, hon." She pecked him on the cheek and laid a pink slip of paper on the desk calendar. He glanced at the notice.

COULD I PLEASE DROP BY FOR A MOMENT TOMORROW AFTERNOON?

WILL K.

Jeff's eyes met hers.

"You think?" he asked.

"It wouldn't surprise me."

Jeff rubbed his eyes, looking tired. "Not now," he said to no one in particular. "Please, not now."

The following afternoon Will Kindberg, Colombian branch director and personal friend, sat in a rocking chair in the Smothermons' living room.

"Now," he began. The athletic man in his fifties bore his usual pleasant look, but discomfort also etched his face. "Jeff and Jo, I really don't know how to ask this. Be open as I talk. Say 'no' if you can't do it, but prayerfully consider before turning me down."

Jeff and his wife sat together on the couch looking as nervous as they felt.

"Something has come up that you probably won't want to do," continued Will.

Jeff felt his throat tighten.

"It's about Bogota. We desperately need two people there—one to manage the guest–house, one to take the buyer's job."

Jeff's heart sank.

"We do have someone considering the guest house position now. Nothing definite, just a possibility. But as far as the buyer's job, we're dry."

"Will," Jeff began.

"Hear me out," Will interrupted, holding up his hand. "I didn't come to you two without a lot of thought. Nor did I come to you first. I've exhausted a list of possibilities a mile long. No one else can do it." He paused. "No one."

The young couple sat. Jo expelled a breath as if short of air. Without looking up she asked the director, "Do you know about the goal we're shooting for?"

"The fifty-percent thing?"

"Uh, huh," she replied. "Half of the New Testament translated before our furlough six months from now. We didn't make that commitment lightly."

"I realize that."

"There's another factor, too," added Jeff.
"We're sitting on some literacy primers we've just got to check out with the Macunas once more before they go to print. A six-month stretch in Bogota would make that impossible."

Will's face was pained. "I've tried everything," he said. "I've asked everyone I could think of. I've thought of alternatives—even considered having the guest-house manager take the buyer's job, too. But it's too mammoth a task." He paused. "You know how I hate to pull translators off their assignments. If there was any way I could do the job with support people, I would."

The remark hit home. Will was telling the truth. All awkward silence followed.

"We don't like the idea but we'll think and pray about it for a few days. Okay?"

Will nodded. "That's all I can ask."

For the next several days all Jeff could see before him was the dismal warehouse in the capital city a hundred and ten miles away. The buyer who ran it was the lifeblood of Lomalinda. Every item sold in the store, every Honda and radio part, the ink, the gas, the paper clips—every last product imaginable from cement blocks to violin strings was ordered by the buyer and came through that warehouse to the workers and their families.

It was a crucial job . . . for somebody. But he was a linguist. He had studied for years so he could translate the Bible into Macuna. Of course, all the translators had to take their turn at service jobs. There just weren't enough support people to fill the slots. But the Smothermons had already done a service stint when they first came to South America. And now was the worst possible time for a situation like this.

Despite his anguish Jeff did not feel free to share his predicament with anyone until he had responded to Will. He didn't even confide in his good friend Chet when they bumped into each other at the store the following afternoon.

'Say, Jeff, you think you and Jo could pray about something for Brenda and me? I've been asked to manage the guest house in Bogota for six months or so. You know how itching we are to get to a tribe. We're not sure whether to take it or not."

"You didn't get your tribal assignment, did you?" asked Jeff.

"No. Just want to be ready in case."

Jeff stifled the urge to relate his own tale of woe and agreed to pray for the Bittermans to make a wise decision. But the following Sunday the Bittermans sat by the Smothermons in church, and that afternoon they ran into each other again at the lake with their children. Jeff's heaviness could remain inside no longer. He told Chet about the incident with Will.

Chet looked incredulous. "You? You guys have been with a tribe since before Columbus, and they asked you?"

Three days later a nervous Jeff Smothermon picked up the phone and dialed the director's office. They had thought, they had prayed, they had cried. They couldn't do it. They had a commitment to keep. Will was in a bind and they knew it, but there was just nothing they could do. They only hoped, that . . . .

"Hello. Will Kindberg."

"Will?"

"Yes."

"Jeff Smothermon, here." Jeff was shaking and· spoke quickly. "Will, we've thought a lot about what you asked us. We've prayed a lot, too. We've wrestled and wrestled—"

"Jeff?"

Jeff stopped. "Yes?"

"Jeff, you don't have to give me an answer. You don't have to do anything. Chet Bitterman was in my office this morning. He and Brenda learned about your situation and after thinking it through, Chet offered to take the buyer's job in addition to his own. He said it would be a shame to pull you off right now. He said he'd do anything to keep you on the field."

Jeff was stunned. "But those are two full-time jobs," he protested.

"I know," answered Will. "But he wants to try. "

Jeff thanked Will and hung up the phone. "Jo," he called. "Come here. I've got to tell you something. "

He had never been so grateful. His friend Chet had broad shoulders.

An Omen

High on an Andean plateau, eighty-six hundred feet above sea level, sprawls the city of Bogota—hugging the mountain base, four million strong. When not enveloped in clouds, its skyscrapers can be seen imitating the mountain peaks, stretched toward the sky. Surrounding the business district, mile after mile of Spanish-style, red tile roofs glisten in the sun.

Culture, as well as drizzly cold weather, sets the city apart from the steamy lowlands. Bogota exudes sophistication. Three-piece suits and stylish dresses are standard attire; the only jeans. come designer made. Here, Bronkies sells its world-famous emeralds, the Gold Museum displays pre-Colombian artifacts to a quarter million visitors yearly and prestigious universities flourish. It is the Athens of Latin America.

On January 2, 1980, Chet Bitterman and his family arrived from Lomalinda at Bogota's EI Dorado Airport. They were met in the terminal by a Wycliffe lady, a poster of Juan Valdez (who picks only the richest and ripest coffee beans), and a warning not to wear watches, jewelry, or wallets in the streets if they wished to keep them for long. Hailing a cab they negotiated a price and sped northward.

Bogota's nicer suburbs lay northward. For security reasons. SIL had moved its guest-house there to a quiet neighborhood two years earlier. Nothing about the white, two-story townhouse stood out from the rest of the street. But its corner location provided twice the usual parking space plus entrance from two sides. Chet and Brenda rented a home close by.

The north did have its disadvantages. The warehouse and administrative offices remained downtown, a forty-five minute drive away. This meant longer days. With two jobs, longer days would soon become the last thing Chet needed.

"Hey, hey, what's up?" Chet bounced through the guest house door with his boyish smirk, spitting out Spanish small talk. The maids at the stove grinned. He sniffed the coffee pot and snatched. a strip of bacon. "What's a great cook like you doing in a place like this?"

Stepping into the side office that doubled as a laundry room, he checked the telex for overnight messages: phone so and so . . . arrange such and such . . . Wheeler's flight okayed, but could return be delayed? He would check with Al that afternoon, downtown. He ripped the sheet from the machine and started through the house to the rear office.

"Morning, Chet."

One of the pilots spoke from behind the morning paper. Did Chet know the house car had a flat? That the spare was also flat? And that Charles Jenkins needed a ride downtown?

Chet would cover it.

He scanned his desk. Payments to enter. Salaries to pay. A note to himself from last week: schedule doctor's appointment for Zechiels this Thursday. An airport run at 8:30. He'd almost forgotten.

The phone rang. It was Bob Whitesides, SIL public relations man downtown. Yes, he remembered they were on for lunch today at Wimpy's. Chet hung up the phone and flipped through his mail. Reservation request, reservation request, dental appointment request—he'd have to translate that one for Nelly and have her call it in later. This job had certainly stretched his Spanish. Electric bill, purchase order.... ah, here was one from a friend in Lomalinda, a welcome break from the business mail.

> Chet,
> How are you doing? Listen, the kids wanted to make a corsage for their mom's birthday. We know you are terribly busy but I was wondering if, as a favor, you could get hold of some ribbons and pins and—

Chet growled. Brother! This was a bad place to be when you had friends living sixty miles from the nearest paved road. When would he ever find time to track down all this stuff?

A verse from St. Paul flashed to his mind. *Do not merely look out for your own personal interests, but also for the interests of others.* He checked himself. "Got you, Lord." For the past several years he had memorized Scripture daily. Sometimes, like today, it got rather personal.

Chet stuffed the letter in his pocket, translated the dental request, told Charles to meet him in the van in fifteen minutes, found an extra spare in the garage, asked a visiting linguist to cover for him at the airport, changed the tire, threw the two flat tires into the rear of the van, and plopped into the driver's seat.

Beside Chet sat Charles, collapsed in the passenger seat, his head resting against the window. Chet gunned the engine and threw the van into gear.

"Well, Charles, my boy, it's good to have you." He halted at the end of the side street, then plunged into Suba Avenue, the main boulevard. "How's the wife and kids?"

Charles held his head in his hand. "Boy, I'm sick."

"Sorry you're feeling bad." Chet weaved in and out of traffic. "I'll pray for you."

Charles eyed him through parted fingers.

"No, really," said Chet. The low buildings of the city whizzed by.

"You know, Charles, the drive downtown takes forty-five minutes under normal conditions. Of course, I've never seen conditions normal." Chet laughed at his own comment. Charles said nothing.

"A Colombian told me the traffic signs down here are as negotiable as the prices. A yellow light doesn't mean anything. And stop signs and red lights are just general guidelines. He said if you don't have two or three near-misses a day you're not driving well."

A car in the right lane shot in front of their van to turn left. Chet jammed the brakes and swerved around, the pace of his chatter barely slackening. Charles opened his window. "At a red light you start easing out into the street or the traffic will never let you in." Problem is, you can't see the light because you're under it. You know it's green when the horns behind you start honking."

Charles's head dropped between his knees as Chet mumbled something about eye contact being the key at intersections.

Two-thirds of the way downtown traffic jammed up for blocks at a corner where the light was out. A puzzled cow stared at the confusion from an overgrown lot between elegant houses. Chet grew impatient, stepped onto the street and began directing vehicles—haggling with the more obstinate drivers. In ten minutes the horns fell silent as traffic moved again. Charles shook his head in disbelief at the American who was more Colombian than the Colombians.

Finally they reached the center of the city where the streets became macadam canyons between office buildings. Charles tumbled out of the van and waved a thank you to his driver who was concluding a discussion of Latin politics.

"It's been real, Chet," he managed to say. Chet nodded and barreled off.

Minutes later, his van parked, Chet strode into the lobby of the towering Ministry of Government Building. SIL worked under the Government Minister and was therefore provided office space in the building on the seventh and eighth floors. The Minister must be in, thought Chet, noting the number of security guards. Chet glanced at his corduroys and sports shirt; he wished he had worn his suit.

"I'll expect you at 7:00. You'll bring your wife?"

Behind him Chet overheard the Spanish conversation of two approaching gentlemen.

"Fine. 7:00. Colombian or gringo time?"

Chet recognized the voice and humor of Al Wheeler, SIL office administrator. Good. He could enter on the older man's coattails. The doctor of linguistics had taken leave of his jungle tribe several years earlier to fill the office position. He spent the hours before breakfast at a bedroom desk revising his Siona New Testament.

The elevator filled and began its ascent. Secretaries and polite officials tried to conceal their awe at the height and shoe size of the silver-haired American. "They're fourteens," smiled Al, easing the tension.

Inside the office Chet tackled paperwork, then made phone calls. He needed to get the fuel tanker out early—mountain roads in the direction of

Lomalinda were reported washed out. He needed an appointment with the Ministry of Health to approve more anti-venom for snake bites. He needed an aluminum strip for a radio antennae—perhaps Publio would know where to look. He'd need help locating a part for the printing press. He needed . . . .

"Ready, Chet?"

It was Bob Whitesides. Chet glanced at his watch. Where had the morning gone? He phoned the warehouse to tell Publio he'd be in at two, then headed out with his friend for quarter pounders and cokes.

* * *

Two miles west of the Ministry Building, richer fare was being served reception guests at the Dominican Republic Embassy. It was February 27, Dominican Independence Day. Cocktails in hand, the ambassadors of fifteen nations and their entourages exchanged small talk and sampled hors d'oeuvres.

By 11:45 the Soviet Ambassador and Eastern bloc envoys had paid their respects and left. The new East German Ambassador, they explained, was having his credentials presented elsewhere in the city and their presence was expected.

Outside the embassy all traffic scurried by at its usual pace and some young people kicked a soccer ball in afield at the National University across the street. Two well-dressed, unidentified young couples stood in the doorway. No one paid attention: gate-crashers were common fixtures at Colombian diplomatic receptions.

About noon, U.S. Ambassador Diego Asencio excused himself and started toward the door where his armored Chrysler Imperial limousine awaited. Suddenly the two young couples pulled pistols from their jackets and fired at the ceiling. Simultaneously, the soccer players across the street produced shotguns and other weapons from their gym bags and stormed the embassy gates.

Two hours later one attacker lay dead, four policemen and a bodyguard had been wounded, and the terrorists commanded the compound.

The news spread quickly along Bogota's streets. By the time Chet and Bob returned to the office they had pieced together most of the radio bulletin's information.

> The men and women occupying the building have identified themselves as members of the April 19 Movement, popularly known as M-19.

Chet's eyes met Bob's. This was the same publicity-grabbing group that in 1976 had murdered anticommunist labor leader Jose Mercado Martinez. They were no-nonsense types.

> Many will recall the group's daring theft of over 5,000 rifles in January, 1979, when they tunneled under the city's army munitions depot. The arms were later recovered in a government dragnet that resulted in the arrest of more than 400 suspects, at which time many believed the underground organization effectively shattered.

The SIL office staff listened with awe to the accounts of the urban terrorist group's successful exploits.

The gunmen hold an estimated fifty hostages, among them fifteen ambassadors. Calling himself "Commander One," the group's spokesman warned that his colleagues would begin executing the hostages as a security measure if soldiers and riot police did not withdraw. Says the leader, "We're prepared to stay here one or two months if necessary."—You are listening to Radio Todelar.

That evening during the city's nightly energy-conservation blackout, Chet and Brenda roasted marshmallows in their fireplace as they followed the news update on a battery transistor. The announcer broadcast the terrorist demands:

— $50 million in ransom

— release of 311 political prisoners (many of them M-19, on trial for murder, kidnapping, and armed robbery)

— international publication of a manifesto exposing alleged repression in Colombia

— safe passage out of the country

Brenda moaned in disgust as she thought of the captives' spouses and children.

"What would you do, Chet, if you were President Turbay?"

"I think he should stick to his guns," he answered, popping a marshmallow into his mouth.

"But what about the ambassadors?"

Chet leaned back in his chair. "You hate to hurt people, but it'd be better to sacrifice a few lives if necessary than give in to these jokers and encourage them to do it again."

Brenda nodded.

The weeks wore on as government-terrorist

negotiations continued in a panel truck outside the embassy. From time to time sick or insignificant hostages were released as gestures of good will. But progress crawled. Americans, in particular, found the ordeal demoralizing—their diplomats in Iran had been held by Islamic revolutionaries since the past November.

Through March and into April, Chet's and Brenda's personal lives took on the same wearisome tone as the negotiations. Guest house and buyer's job responsibilities drained them. Hard-to-fill orders poured in. Shipments arrived late. The supposed forty-five-minute trip downtown—already an hour and a half due to rush-hour traffic—grew longer as security detours around the Dominican Embassy forced Chet through the city's most congested area. Some evenings on his drive home, the energy blackout hit as Chet sat at a red light. Instantly cars from every direction would pour into the intersection.

By the time he pulled up to his house, his nerves were usually shot.

On April 27 an agreement was reached in the Dominican Embassy standoff. M-19 accepted a promised $2.5 million in private ransom, plus government assurances of internationally monitored trials for the prisoners in question. Fifteen terrorists and their dozen remaining hostages, all ambassadors, boarded a Cubana Airlines jet for Havana.

Chet wished he were aboard. "I'm ready to get out of here," he told Bob over lunch, anxious to trade city pressures and his coat and tie for the challenge of the jungle. In five weeks his assignment would be over.

But not his problems.

Three weeks before returning to Lomalinda Chet's van collided with a police captain's car downtown. One passenger claimed injury, and by law Chet was held in confinement and both vehicles impounded.

"Tiene derecho para una llamada." The guard repeated the words but Chet's Spanish deserted him. The stature of his legal opponent plus the impact of the collision had left him shaken. He was alone and frightened.

"You may make one phone call," someone finally made him understand, and Chet dialed Brenda with a borrowed coin.

Late that night he walked out of jail and by noon the next day both vehicles were released. But the damage was done and the court proceedings promised to drag on for months, perhaps years.

On June 3, 1980, his trial still pending, the spent administrator boarded an SIL plane for Lomalinda to join his family who had left the week before. The Smothermons, whose buyer's job he had taken, were now on furlough and in gratitude had left their home, rent-free, for the Bittermans' use.

"It's going to be nice," Chet said to himself, settling into the seat. He just knew he would soon be among the Carabayos. He was wrong.

The Size of the Fight
in the Dog

Squeezing more rpm's from his Honda 90 than the tired machine wanted to give, Chet Bitterman flew down the footpath that fell steeply from Lomalinda's post office. One-year-old Esther was strapped to his back in a Gerry Carrier. Vehicles weren't supposed to use the footpaths; but today he was behind schedule. Chet was usually behind schedule.

Puddles lay across the way but the downpour was almost over and shafts of sunlight poked through the clouds. Emerald plains, baptized in gold, stretched as far as the eye could see.

The beauty did not catch Chet's eye. His mind was elsewhere. It was in the austere courthouse back in. Bogota where he must soon return for a third traffic hearing. It was in the jungle with the Carabayos, aching for government permission to enter with his family. It was over at the store stacking clothes pins and canned goods—trying to be content.

He raced up a hill past the volleyball court and mounted the crest. The Smothermons' house lay ahead, commanding a wide view of the countryside. Nice of them to offer their place, he thought. Still, he and Brenda needed a place of their own. The bike skidded to a stop that sent stones flying. Chet kicked down the stand and strode quickly toward the door.

"I'm home, Babes. Brought the chickie from "nursery."

He entered the empty kitchen and fished in the refrigerator for a carrot.

"Can't stay for lunch. I promised the folks in Port I'd have that swing set up by tonight."

No one answered.

Chet straightened up and closed the door. "Anna? Brenda?" He poked his head into each room. From the living room he peered through the screen door to the outdoor pantry where his wife and daughter knelt over a woven basket. Brenda's arm encircled Anna. Anna was sobbing.

Chet nudged open the door. In the basket lay Pretty Bird, the Bitterman's parrot, a green and blue patch under his motionless head, a bright yellow spot under his unblinking eye. The chubby-faced little girl could not understand why her winged friend wasn't out in the cashew tree, flitting from limb to limb. Her shoulders rose and fell in spasms of sorrow.

"Why don't you take Esther?" Chet said to Brenda. He unstrapped the infant from his back and knelt beside Anna. Pulling her head to his chest, he combed his fingers through her locks. They sat.

"Pretty Bird's dead, Angel," he finally said. The girl spoke through her sniffles. "I don't want him to be dead."

"I know, 1 don't either. Come on, we'll bury him."

"In the dirt?"

Chet nodded. He slid his fingers under the bird. "Would you like to hold him?" He placed Pretty Bird into her cupped hands, reached for a shovel, and together the two stepped onto the lawn and started up the slope.

No pallbearer ever discharged his duties with more gentleness than the misty-eyed little girl who marched in procession with her father that afternoon. They stopped at the grass's edge. Chet dug a small hole, then two undersized hands lay Pretty Bird into his final nest.

Chet stooped to hug his daughter. Her dress hem soaked up the water droplets that clung to the blades of grass. The air smelled of damp earth. Chet struggled for words.

"You know, everything has to die sometime, Angel."

Only bug noises from the weeds replied.

"The trees, this grass, those flowers over there—they'll all die sometime. Animals die, too. God gives them a good long life and then they die." Anna stared silently.

"Pretty Bird had a lot of fun for a long time. He liked you, didn't he?"

She gave a slow nod.

"Did you know that people die, too? They do. Usually God lets them live a good long life and then they die. Everyone will."

Chet had no idea how much she understood. "When a person dies we put his body into the ground, just like Pretty Bird. It's like he's going to sleep. It's like when mama and papa put you in your bed at night." Chet paused to think again. "But dying is not something we need to be afraid of, anymore than going to sleep is. Because even if our bodies go inside the ground, our souls don't. They're still alive. Do you know what a soul is?" Chet stroked her hair.

"Your soul is inside you. You can't see it or feel it. But it's there. It's the real you, the real Anna Ruth. Your soul is what makes you laugh when you're happy and cry when you're sad. It's what makes you love Pretty Bird."

A soundless grief returned to Anna's face. Chet wiped her eyes.

"When a person dies his soul stays alive even if his body lies in the ground. He can still hear and see. And best of all, for people who love Jesus, their souls go to be with him in heaven. Heaven is the neatest place anywhere. Do you remember mama and me talking to you about heaven?"

Another slow nod. Chet and Brenda frequently read to the girls from the Bible.

"Heaven is a place for Jesus and his friends. That's why mama and I and you girls are here in Colombia—so we can tell the Indians about Jesus and they can be with him in heaven." He pulled her head close. "Anna, you'll go to heaven someday if you love Jesus."

Chet rested his chin on her head and together they rocked side to side, staring at the bird. As if a thought had come to her, Anna stopped still.

"Is Pretty Bird in heaven?" She turned and looked at Chet.

"Anna," he said, "when you get to heaven, if you need Pretty Bird there to be happy . . . he'll be there." The girl pondered this statement, then sat back in Chet's arms. He cradled her, and sang hymns to her, as he often did. When she was ready Chet covered the bird with dirt and they trudged back toward the house.

Minutes later Chet sped out of the drive. He'd be cutting through some footpaths to save time. Vehicles weren't supposed to use the footpaths but today he was behind schedule.

The shooting took place their first night back from vacation.

Vacation had been great. Nothing to do but swim and lounge about in that rustic town by the Brazilian border. The low dive of the motel pool still called to them as they boarded the plane for home.

What a shock the return arrival had been.

Scarcely had the landing gear scraped the runway dirt before Chet and Brenda could see soldiers from the windows. Soldiers at Lomalinda! Barefoot children scampered alongside the marching columns, their little eyes fixed upon loaded rifles and hand grenades.

Brenda shuddered.

That evening George and Joan Gardner came to the Bittermans' for popcorn and to explain the soldiers' presence. Word was, they said, that the army had gotten wind of attacks planned against the center. The village of Puerto Lleras (called "Port"), four miles away, and SIL's training farm across the swamp were in danger, too. A local fellow in league with rural guerrillas had gone to the army and blown the whistle. Apparently the army wanted more information, so instead of whisking the man away they sent him back to glean what he could. But the guerrillas grew suspicious. The spy, fearing he had been discovered, fled to the army officials.

"We'll get you out of the area," the commandant assured him, "someplace you won't be found."

But the terrified man insisted he would be hunted down no matter where he went. He was certain they would kill his family who were left behind.

They didn't have to. The next day the man shot himself on the street in Port.

Brenda was still trying to grasp the reality of it all when the alarm siren sounded that night.

"Chet, did you hear that?"

Chet lay beside her in bed, propped up on a pillow, his attention divided between the radio news and his *Time* magazine.

"Hear what?"

"The siren . . . I think."

"Nah, your folks got you too psyched up tonight."

"Chet, I'm sure that's the alarm."

Chet realized his wife's concern and went to investigate. So, someone killed himself. He was sorry. But wasn't everyone overreacting just a bit? Eleven to five curfew. Dogs tied up at night. Staggered schedule for public meetings. Vehicles into Port by two's only—close enough to see each other but not so close to be captured together if attacked.

Chet unscrewed the outside light bulbs, locked the door, carried the children into the bedroom with him and Brenda, and turned off the radio. That should make her happy.

As his head hit the pillow they heard the shooting.

In his dark home in another part of the center, branch director Will Kindberg picked up the phone. It was dead. He glanced at the alarm clock on his nightstand. Dead. They'll come for me, he thought. I'm the director. Methodically he dressed himself and set out a back pack of clothes and medicine. His task accomplished, he swallowed dryly and lay down to wait.

Dawn came. Will slumbered beside his wife and daughter. Dogs stretched, monkeys romped, parrots squawked. Pink sunlight stroked the lake. Shooting and terrorists and automatic rifles seemed far away. No one was hurt.

The previous night's events began, piecing together as phone lines buzzed once again. Unidentified assailants, faceless in the dark, had opened fire on the training farm in three separate attacks.

Government troops had responded in kind. At the commandant's order the alarm had been sounded and Lomalinda's generator shut down to insure a blackout.

Word began circulating that a kidnapping might better meet terrorist hopes of ousting SIL than a frontal assault. An abduction would entail no killing, no muss, no fuss. Just maximum results with minimum bad publicity.

Every diary in Lomalinda painted a different picture of the terrorist threat those next two weeks. Brenda penned her fears in scarlet; Chet wrote in business-as-usual gray. What was there to worry about? A bunch of hotheaded rabble rousers were no match for an organized detachment of troops. Life would continue as usual: up at 5:30, devotions, pray for the Carabayos, fry eggs for the girls, bike to work, think about the Carabayos, home for lunch, memorize Scripture (the Carabayos would like this verse!), back to work, daydream about Carabayos, volleyball, supper, dessert at Gardners and talk about the Carabayos, put the girls to bed, plan about contacting Carabayos, pray together for Carabayos, fall asleep thinking about Carabayos . . . .

"Brenda?"

Chet's voice came across flat over the radio patch. Bogota was a hundred and ten miles northwest; he sounded a continent away.

"Honey?" Brenda frowned. "You don't sound well. Did the trial go poorly? Over."

"It's still up in the air."

"Was the lawyer there? Is he handling things? Over."

"Yeah."

"Are you worn out from it all? Over."

"A bit. That's neither here nor there."

"Then what's happening, Chet?"

"Brenda . . . I was at the Ministry of Government today . . . ."

"Yes? Chet?"

"We can't go to the tribe, Brenda. Too many outsiders want in. Over."

Brenda clicked off the microphone in disbelief and sank into the chair. The Carabayo project was over.

* * *

"It's not the size of the dog in the fight but the size of the fight in the dog." Chet had quoted the phrase a hundred times in high school and college. He still believed it. The Carabayo project was over? All right. He would find another. Meanwhile, God could be trusted to care for the Carabayos.

He turned to the "Tribes to be Entered" files in the Technical Studies Department. Together he and Brenda researched the few remaining "mystery tribes," groups that outsiders had rarely contacted. Two criteria guided them as they scoured each thin folder: do these people still use their own language, and will they be using it ten years' from now? The inroads of Spanish made answers uncertain.

One by one names fell from the list. Plains tribes were scratched; jungle tribes remained. Obscure tongues survived over near cousins of known languages. The tougher the assignment, the better.

"Are you thinking what I'm thinking?" Chet asked his wife as the time for decision neared.

The two stared at the brown folder on the table. CARIJONA, read the label.

"I think so," she answered.

"I'll ask Wen to survey them with me," said Chet. "He knows what he's doing."

*   *   *

Chet and Wen's flight destination was a tiny riverbank town named Miraflores, deep in the Vaupes jungles. The town had the closest airstrip to any known Carijona settlement. En route, they twice landed in jungle clearings—old rubber hunting grounds—and asked for information about other possible Carijona locations. No one knew anything. They proceeded on to the town.

A dirt airstrip, patrolled by soldiers, cut through the middle of the ramshackle village. Wood-slat buildings with low porches slumped on either side gave the appearance of a Wild West town. Three or four dirt roads branched out perpendicularly from the runway but shortly faded into footpaths and were swallowed by jungle.

Soldiers questioned the linguists. Chet and Wen explained that they were interested in traveling down river to meet Carijonas. They had no contacts but were hoping to find a launch going their way. The sergeant said they should have no problem since boats and planes came and went often. Chet and Wen had noticed this—several DC-3s had landed in the few minutes they had been there. They mentioned it to the sergeant. He grinned. "People have their business."

Chet and Wen walked through the town toward

the river—past a Catholic mission, past little stores carrying everything from chain saws to baking flour, past a bar, pool hall, and a private home where female entrepreneurs attracted a steady clientele. Dust clung to their shoes. The sun turned liquid on their bodies. A cafe sold them cokes for a dollar a piece.

At the riverbank they negotiated a price with a young man whose dugout canoe had a Johnson outboard mounted on the stern.

So much for the cowboy town, thought Chet as they launched off. Now for the Indians.

Within Arms Reach

His name was Carlos. He was blind. He didn't like strangers.

Carlos was boss here. He had lived in this hut on the river for so many years he had lost count. His father the rubber hunter had relocated the Carijonas here decades ago to extract the precious stuff. But times had changed. Old Man Rubber had died with his father. There was another plant now.

Through the night sounds the half-Indian could hear an outboard engine approaching. Sputtering off. Feet sloshing up on the bank and onto his porch.

Men. Language people. Wanting a place for the night. (Friendly. What did they really want?) They could hang their hammocks on the porch. He fell into his own hammock and heard his wife blowout the candle. He hoped the visitors realized that even a blind man can sleep with one eye open.

5:00 A.M. Chet and Wen roll up their hammocks and wait on the porch for the day to begin. Chet inserts his contact lenses.

6:00 A.M. Carlos joins his visitors on the porch. They assure him his business affairs are of no concern to them. A barefoot Indian named Juan appears. Under his shirt he carries a copy of jungle law—a revolver sticking into his pants. He will leave in two minutes for a Carijona settlement that is two hours into the jungle. The blancos may come along.

6:15 A.M. Juan is ahead out of sight. The linguists recall the proverb, "He who walks with an Indian walks alone." Yet there is little danger of losing the path, which is clear. A light drizzle begins. At places the mud on the mule trail is knee deep.

7:30 A.M. An Indian approaches. He has passed Juan, who sends a message: they should take a different trail. No mules travel it; there is less mud. They will find a certain hut—get directions. Travel quickens.

8:00 A.M. Wen has worn the wrong style boots; he can feel them lift the toenails from his toes. He does not mention it, so as not to discourage Chet. The air is warm.

10:15 A.M. No house, only trail after trail after trail.

12:00 noon. Chet and Wen rest on a rock and finish the last of their granola rations. Five men approach on the path carrying pistols and shotguns. They seem uneasy around the unfamiliar blancos. The linguists ask directions. Yes, they have missed their trail. The linguists turn back. The air is very hot.

1:15 P.M. Fatigue and near-depression. The water is gone. Sweltering heat.

2:00 P.M. Someone approaches—the same Indian who sent them on an alternate trail that morning. He directs them home.

4:00 P.M. Chet and Wen stumble into Carlos's clearing, bathe in the river, eat sardines, and collapse into their hammocks. Night soon falls. The next morning the men decided against another inland expedition. Instead, they visited

Carijona huts up and down river. They learned that tile whole tribe would have to meet to approve the Bittermans' coming to live. On Thursday an Indian, motored the linguists back to Miraflores in his fiberglass speedboat. A kind priest shared his quarters that night. To sleep outside, he said, invited danger. On Friday a plane from Lomalinda took them home.

Six weeks later, Chet returned with his family. With them was a friend, Jim, a linguist of sixteen years experience in the Vaupes jungles. Their visit caught Carlos by surprise. He had not gotten their plane-dropped message about when they would be coming.

"Your plane!" the man said. "We thought the police were snooping. Everyone ran and hid in the trees. No one waited to see anything drop."

They could see the man's embarrassment. His wife was away and he could not properly entertain. "I . . . have no food," he protested unconvincingly. "Try the old man in the hut down the river. He'll take you in."

They tried, without success. Exhausted, they trudged back to the blind man's. "We have our own food," they said. "All we need is a place to hang our hammocks." Carlos seemed satisfied.

The next morning Chet, his family, and Jim called on the huts along the river. Surprise met them in every home. No tribal meeting had been planned to discuss the Bittermans' coming to live. One man finally agreed to try to gather some people for the following day. But the next day brought only rain, and not one Carijona.

Chet and Brenda wondered: what should they make of this? On Chet's previous trip Carijona enthusiasm had seemed higher. The people themselves had suggested a meeting. Now, they withdrew. Carlos suggested the linguists try the old man down the river again. When the shower faded Jim and the Bittermans plodded to his hut. As they approached they heard an unfamiliar voice in Spanish. A visitor sat on the porch with several local men.

"Are you a Carijona?" asked Chet from the bottom of the steps.

"Desano," said the stranger.

Jim replied with a Desano greeting. The man's eyes brightened. Never had he met a gringo who spoke his language. Jim explained that he had lived among portions of the Desano population for sixteen years.

"Wait here a minute," Jim motioned with his finger. "I've got something to show you."

Jim ran back to Carlos's hut as Chet and the girls mingled with the others. Soon Jim came sloshing back through the mud, protecting a bulge under his shirt from the sporadic drizzle.

"Take a look at this," he said, producing several thin books, shaking the droplets from his face and hair. The Desano placed a book on his lap and began to page through it. Stick-figure sketches of trees and animals illustrated a simple Desano tale about a man and his three dogs hunting tapir.

"Do you read?" asked Jim.

"Some Spanish."

"Then you can read this. It uses the same letters as Spanish. But the story's in Desano."

The Indian's brow wrinkled. He had never seen his language written. He had no reason to believe it could be written.

Jim urged him. "Go on."

His rough finger found the first syllable, then his lips. There was no comprehension. He sounded the second syllable. A light switched on. A smile sprouted on the weathered face. The man repeated the word and smiled again. His finger moved to the second word.

All other conversation on the porch died as Carijona faces stared at the foreigner whose tongue was a mystery but whose smile spoke volumes.

The smile broke into laughter as the elated Desano recognized more and more of the tale he had known as a boy. "My sister has to see this," he exclaimed. The smiling and laughter spread. The further the man read the more he bellowed. Jim's eyes caught Chet's. A thirst for reading—reading his own language—came over the Desano that afternoon.

And not only over the Desano.

That evening as he squatted on a stool by the fire, the old man from the hut down the river studied Carlos's expression. "You have authority, Don Carlos. You can give the word." His wizened face pled. He laid a hand on the blind man's arm. "Can the language people come?"

Glistening in the sun, a blue and white Helio took off for Lomalinda that next morning. The SIL craft would cruise at 6,000 feet on its home-bound flight to Lomalinda. But the plane could never soar the heights of its passengers spirits. Chet and Brenda gazed with aching joy from the windows. Next time they returned, it would be for twenty years.

From the day Chet and Brenda returned to Lomalinda, life shifted into high gear. Their interest lay with the hundred details that needed attention before a family could move to the jungle. But other items drained their time and energies.

"Chet." Brenda stood in the hallway, the phone in her hand. Frustration crossed, her face. "It's the corporal. Don't let your soup get cold."

Chet slurped another spoonful and reached for

the call. "Aló?. . . . Yes. . . . Are you sure?. . . . How long?. . . . I understand. We'll get on it. . . . Yes, sir." He clicked the receiver down.

"Sewage is backed up at House 3 again. It's a bad time for this. The food truck's coming in at 2:00. I'd better run."

Brenda rolled her eyes.

Four weeks ago Chet had been made security coordinator, a post created months earlier when the military had discovered a marked map of Lomalinda in terrorist hands during an anti-guerrilla raid. She understood why they had asked Chet. He was organized, and his personality suited him for the job. Unlike some, he never felt intimidated striding up to a huddle of troops and diving into conversation. His competence in Spanish matched his confidence around people. The soldiers enjoyed the twice-weekly soccer games against Chet and the SIL men. For them, the lusty, right-wing forward barreling down the field was just another Latino.

But the job had its problems. Keeping forty troops housed, happy, and in line was enough to tax anyone's resources. Guns accidentally discharged in the hangar where the men slept. As the terrorist threat dragged on, the commander—then the soldiers—needed better quarters. Overused water and sewage lines demanded attention. Shipments of food, seldom on schedule, required distribution. Incoming truckloads of relief troops had to be met and oriented, usually at night. November's rain became December's dust, and the pace did not slacken. Time for Carijona preparations had to be snatched at odd hours. Long after the children were in bed Chet would sit up with his father-in-law drawing house plans and mapping out strategy. Uninterrupted meals were rare. The telephone became an enemy.

Some of Chet's biggest headaches came from fellow workers skeptical of the seriousness of the terrorist situation.

"Chet, can't you bend security regs this once? We just want to go on a little cycle ride."

"Sorry I didn't register my visitor, Chet—I simply forgot."

"Do I *have* to have a partner into Port? No one's around to go." News of the December slaying in EI Salvador of four American women—three nuns and a social worker—did not seem to move these people.

On Christmas week SIL's entire Colombian membership descended on Lomalinda for branch conference. Linguists returned from the tribes and Bogota workers flew in from the capital city. For most, conference meant a time of refreshment. For Chet it meant a security nightmare. People were everywhere! Meeting schedules were staggered to avoid predictable patterns. Potential for a kidnapping doubled. Chet found little time to attend the meetings.

Brenda watched the tension work on her husband. She saw it in his eyes as he peered from their house to the entrance gate a hundred yards away, where guards occasionally admitted a vehicle without checking. She heard it in his voice as he spoke in muffled tones over the phone to the commander. "There's more to all this than I thought," he would tell her. She noticed it in the absence of jokes and wisecracks.

Most of all, she felt it in his nighttime spasms of pain.

"Chet, what's wrong?"

On the bed beside her, Chet curled in the fetal position. She glanced at the clock. 2:00 A.M. Similar cramps had attacked him in Bogota. At that time they suspected his pancreas. A shot from the doctor had relieved him.

But the pains returned. Six times between the end of November and early January they pierced his abdomen. He would waken at 2:00 A.M. and thrash about until 4:00 when the hurt grew unbearable. The doctor would come to administer a shot, and Chet would recuperate by the next afternoon.

"It doesn't seem food related," said the center's physician. "I can't allow you to leave for your tribe till you've had it diagnosed and treated. You'll need to go to Bogota."

This was fine for Chet. He was ready to leave Lomalinda, attend to his medical problems, buy his wilderness supplies, and get to the jungle.

On January 10, 1981, the Bittermans boarded an SIL plane for Bogota. Chet had finished dressing as he ran to the hangar. From the DC-3 he could see the study shack in the Smothermons' back yard below. He had left the door open.

Fifty-degree weather greeted them in the capital city. They checked into the familiar guest house and laid out their week.

On Monday Chet saw a doctor. "Clean out your system and return for X-rays on Wednesday," the doctor said. So Chet shopped with Brenda. Food. Soap. Toilet paper. A jungle stockpile.

On Wednesday the injected dye did not show up clearly on the negatives. "We'll try it again," said the doctor. "No food for twenty-four hours."

More shopping. More running. No eating.

Thursday. The doctor. "Your gall-bladder absorbed none of the dye, Señor Bitterman. It's not functioning at all. I'm surprised it hasn't given you more trouble. It'll have to come out." Surgery was set for the following Thursday, January 22—another delay in getting to the tribe.

All day Friday Chet and a friend scoured hardware shops and building supply stores. In the evening, Brenda slipped into Chet's favorite red dress and the two stepped out, alone. They dined at a Chinese restaurant, then strolled along storefronts and sampled park benches. Their meandering took them past a theater. On the marquee above them flashed "The Kidnapping of a President." Brenda shuddered and walked on.

They found themselves ordering dessert in another restaurant. From a low corner platform a musician plucked his harp. The delicate strains reminded Brenda of heaven.

Saturday they shopped. At night they called Pennsylvania and talked with Chet's mother and Grant. The conversation was long and warm. Sunday arrived. After church Brenda cooked lunch at the guest house and the family relaxed. Chet read the paper and chatted with the other guests. He chatted with Hank, the new house manager.

In the evening, the Wycliffe people in the city gathered for singing and prayer. There were about thirty. Al Wheeler, the leader, asked Chet to close. "Lord," Chet prayed, "it's no mistake we're all here in Colombia. You knew the plans of our lives even when we were in our mothers' wombs."

That night Chet and Brenda sang to the girls as they put them to bed. "Brenda, you take the wall side tonight. I want to sleep on the right."

She protested. "Why? I always sleep on the right."

"No, hon. I want to read by the lamp." The lamp was against the door.

✶ ✶ ✶

And so it was that on January 19, 1981, in the quiet minutes before dawn, a young American mother sat on the edge of the bed, rocking her nursing daughter, thinking about her family's busy days ahead. Through a yawn she studied her husband who still lay sleeping, face down, on the other bed—hugging the pillow like a little boy.

She was surprised to hear the doorbell. It was 6:30.

More Callers

One Hour Later

Not far from the guest house, an old bus, scarcely anyone aboard, made its way with spurts and stops up Suba Avenue in the orange of a morning sun. On the left stretched the grassy median; on the right, the houses with their walled-in yards. Berta de Sanchez and her teenage daughter alighted at Diagonal 128-C and started down the quiet side street. The bus belched and resumed its tired trek northward.

"Do you know when they'll be back?"

"I'm not sure," young Patricia answered her mother. "I'll give you a call."

The women started toward the house, several blocks away, where Patricia was to baby-sit. Ahead on the left, about halfway to their destination, sat the SIL guest house where Berta cooked and cleaned six days a week. She enjoyed working there. The folks who came through were friendly and most could speak Spanish even if she could not understand their English.

"Look." She poked Patricia and nodded toward a light blue van parked in front of the guest house with a lone driver. "They must have hired it to help the station wagon with the airport load this morning. Guess a lot of folks came in over the weekend. Glad I'm not cooking today."

The women walked past.

"He sure looks familiar."

"Who, that driver?"

"Yes," answered the maid.

"Familiar from where?"

"I'm not sure, but I've seen him before. It'll bother me till I remember."

The mother and daughter arrived at the townhouse where Patricia would spend the morning. As they turned up the sidewalk Berta stopped short. "El lago!" she exclaimed. "I saw him at the lake in Lomalinda over Christmas." She had cooked for branch conference at the center three weeks earlier.

"Are you sure?" Patricia was skeptical. Why would anyone not connected with SIL, make the ten-hour drive to so remote an area?

"He was with local folks who came in the afternoon for a swim. Maybe he has relatives. I know I saw him."

The door opened and they were invited in. Ten minutes later Berta came out alone. She turned up the street in the direction of the bus stop.

As she neared the guest house the van pulled away with its passengers. Ahead of it, laden with what looked like luggage, led the house station wagon. Chet Bitterman was driving. She watched the vehicles scurry up the street and stop where the road made a T at Suba Avenue. To her surprise the station wagon turned north; the opposite direction from the airport. The van turned south.

Two odd things this morning, she thought: the man from the lake and the car turning north. Reaching the guest house she turned up the sidewalk toward the porch. She had the day off, but while she was in the neighborhood, why not pick up her paycheck? She rang the bell.

"Shhh!" The sound came from inside. Berta placed her ear against the door. She was certain she could hear a woman weeping. It sounded like Helena, one of the other maids. Dear Lord, she thought, what's wrong?

She rang again. Nothing.

The puzzled woman walked around, to the side door and rang. Not a sound. By now the street had begun to stir, making the stillness of the house even stranger. Why were the curtains all drawn?

Berta walked briskly across the street and through a playground to the tiny neighborhood grocery. She requested the phone and dialed the guest house. The phone rang and rang.

Scared and uncertain, she dashed back across the street to the house. Nelly, another employee, was just arriving.

"Nelly!" She reached the front steps and with pounding heart described what had happened. "Something bad's going on."

"Don't scare me like this," said Nelly. They knocked and rang but all was still. Berta cupped her hands and stood on tiptoe by the curtained window. "Helena," she hollered.

"Go away!" a woman snapped from inside. The voice was Helena's.

This time Berta and Nelly ran to the store together and asked for the phone. They dialed the downtown office and nervously told Bob Whitesides what had happened. He directed them to the home of Burkhard Schottelndreyer, an SIL translator who lived just blocks away. Ten minutes later the ladies found themselves in Burkhard's living room pouring out the morning's events. A Wycliffe pilot, Gerry Gardner, joined them at Bob's request. The two men garnered the facts as best they could, then pondered their options. Burkhard spoke.

"What do you think, Ger?"

"Well, something's definitely wrong. I tried to radio from my place after not getting through by phone. Got nothing. No phone, no radio, no answer at the door except for craziness."

"What about the police?"

"Yeah, but what would we tell them? We don't have anything concrete."

They debated and prayed. Finally they decided to return and check once more before risking a false alarm. They got in Gerry's car and drove past the guest-house twice. There was nothing. It was agreed upon that the ladies would go to the adjacent house and see what they could learn. The men, who might seem to pose a threat, would keep watch from a half block away on either side.

Cautiously, the women shuffled up to the door. A man answered their knock. Had he heard any strange noises next door? No, he hadn't. No, wait . . . yes, there had been something. Some sort of crash early that morning. But that was all. Yes, that was all. Certainly. The ladies were very welcome. The door closed.

Berta and Nelly reported to Burkhard, who signaled Gerry. Reluctant but determined, the four crept up to the guest house staying close to the walls to avoid being seen. Stealthily they tried doors and eavesdropped at windows. Faint conversation could be heard inside. They risked a knock. Immediately the voices died.

That was enough. The detectives hopped into their car and sped to the police. Several minutes later four policemen returned with them, parking a block away. As the officers carefully approached the house, Burkhard noticed a man's face in the window, peering out through parted curtains. Their eyes met and the curtains fell shut.

Seconds before the police reached the front door, a green sedan raced up to the house. Doors flew open and men dressed in suits and ties emerged with submachine guns. One carried a walkie-talkie. The police seemed to recognize the newcomers. Together they strode to the front door and rang the bell. It was eleven o'clock.

"Abran la puerta! Somos el DAS."

From behind the door a man replied, "No, sir. Let's see your I.D."

The man on the porch held up his weapon before the peep hole. "No es esto prueba suficiente?"

"No, it's not enough. We want an I.D."

The caller produced his card and the door swung open.

For the second time that morning strangers poured into the house. Burkhard and Gerry followed behind them, the maids at their heels. Brenda and the others summed up what had happened, then the house buzzed with life as the investigators surveyed the rooms and leveled questions.

Gerry was appalled at the mess. Bedding and clothes were strewn everywhere and boxes had toppled to the floor. The library was ransacked. Trying to ease the tension the pilot made a joke about sloppy housekeeping. No one laughed.

In the living room officials questioned the residents. Was anybody hurt? What exactly had happened? Where? How many were there? One was a woman? What did they look like? What did they wear? More men arrived with cameras and typewriters. The house took on the appearance of a newspaper editorial room: Keys tapped and bulbs flashed. Phone calls came in continuous, streams. Families were notified; downtown was notified. Bolts secured the doors—admittance only by recognition. A lieutenant ordered bodyguards for Al Wheeler and roadblocks erected all over Bogota. Gerry left to radio Lomalinda.

Brenda's head swam from the battery of questions. Certainly, she understood they were necessary. The men from F-2 needed to know. F-2: National Police Intelligence. Describe that again, you say? Well, it was like this . . . . Oh no, another man with paper and pencil. Yes, I'm the wife of Señor Bitterman. Yes, of course, DAS: Department of Internal Security. Yes, certainly, you need to ask a few questions. Could you please repeat that? (It's so hard to think Spanish at a time like this.) B-2? Military Intelligence. But I've already answered these questions for DAS. Yes, forgive me, you need this to help. There were seven. Middle twenties. Here's a recent photo of my husband. I don't know about that, you'll have to ask the others. Pardon? You wish to introduce me to Señor So-and-So? From CAES? Please, I don't know if I can go through this again. (Father, help me.)

The inquisitors produced books. For the next several hours Brenda and the others sat flipping through pages of mug shots on the coffee table. It was a process that would last several days. In time the hundreds of photographs blended into each other. One man's moustache attached itself to another's lip. Brenda blinked. The curve of their brows and the shape of their cheekbones seemed to melt before her gaze, hardening into one composite face. The anguished woman turned from the book, her eyes weary and blurred with tears.

* * *

The news came at 4,500 feet for the director-elect of SIL's Colombian branch. Nestled in a single engine Helio, he and his two companions, felt their stomachs tighten at the report on the short wave.

The three had planned a public relations visit with local officials in the city of Villavicencio, halfway between Bogota and Lomalinda. Now their plans changed. Landing in Villavicencio they met Will Kindberg, current branch director, and sped to a meeting of top security chiefs and military commanders. The council placed security restrictions on SIL effective immediately: no land travel outside of Lomalinda, increased military protection, landing of SIL aircraft in Villavicencio restricted to the military airport. Later that day the delegation flew home to Lomalinda, touching down en route to pick up the military colonel in charge of the area. Late into the night the colonel and Wycliffe officials sat up with local police discussing strategy. The close subtropical air did not relieve the chill.

* * *

During the blackout that evening in Bogota, Brenda and the others sat huddled around the fireplace, their pensive faces lit with a flickering orange hue. Every so often someone broke the silence.

"I thought this afternoon when they found the abandoned car—" one man began, then paused. "I just knew they'd find some clues."

They didn't.

The group talked, prayed, and sang hymns. Mostly, though, they just thought back over the day, especially the kidnapping itself and the three-hour wait afterward. . . .

When the abductors shut the door that morning the group had remained still for a few minutes, fearful that the terrorists might be listening outside. Finally someone had whispered, "Hey, why doesn't one of the mothers get a knife from the kitchen and cut us free?" No one had bound the feet of the women with children.

"I'm already untied," announced Pete Manier, holding up his palms to the surprise of his companions. The terrorists had failed to re-tie him after his return from the radio room. Now he produced a pocket knife. Soon everyone was stretching and massaging aching wrists and ankles. One lady's hands had been so tightly bound she wondered if she would ever use them again. Fred Gross recalled that he had undergone leg surgery a year ago to the day: the cramp in his leg would not let him forget.

People scattered throughout the house to take stock of their losses. As Helena scrambled eggs for breakfast, Fred slipped unnoticed to the side office and hooked up the phones. May as well be ready for a quick call out when the three hours are up, he thought. Not that waiting three hours was the unanimous opinion. Some felt the police should be called immediately: why give the terrorists a huge head start and guarantee their getaway? Others said that disobeying orders might increase the danger to Chet's life. What if the phones were tapped, or the house was being watched? But Brenda was adamant. No calling—it could mean Chet's death. Out of fear for Chet and deference to Brenda a consensus emerged: sit tight till eleven o'clock.

But sitting tight was not always easy. The ringing of the doorbell proved an enormous temptation for some. If friends stood outside, why not open to them? When Berta yelled from outside, the urge became almost unbearable.

"Go away!" Helena had shouted back. Immediately several of the group nearly pounced on her for fear she was endangering Chet's life.

Once, the phone rang. One of the children, too young to understand the situation, answered. Pete grabbed the receiver and placed it to his ear. The downtown office spoke on the other end. "Hello? What's wrong? Hello?" He replaced the receiver without a word. Some, unaware that Fred had rehooked the phone, became angry, fearful that someone had tried to call out.

At another point one of the men spread the curtains to peer out. Others thought this to be incredibly careless. The air turned electric with nervous tension, each person feeling regret the moment he or she uttered a harsh word. Some asked forgiveness for snapping so quickly and others wept at their own feeling of helplessness. They talked, they sang, they joined hands and bowed in prayer together. . . .

Someone began the first line of a hymn. Brenda looked up from the fireplace and realized it was evening. She joined in the song, looking around the room at her fellow workers. They were friends, they loved each other. God forgive them. God help them. God be with Chet.

They ended the hymn and went to bed.

✳ ✳ ✳

The next forty-eight hours brought a feeling of obscurity. Chet disappeared on Monday, January 19. Tuesday eclipsed the kidnapping with two events that led to a *Time* cover story about "America's Incredible Day." Shortly before noon, Eastern Standard Time, Ronald Reagan was inaugurated fortieth president of the United States to a twenty-one gun howitzer salute and accompaniment of the U.S. Marine Band. Almost simultaneously an Air Algerie 707 lifted from Mehrabad airport in Teheran with fifty-two American hostages soaring toward freedom.

The media focused on little else.

> *NEWSWEEK* It was Day 444 and Day One come together in rare historic symmetry the end of the long ordeal of the hostages in Iran and the beginning of what Reagan promised could be "an era of national renewal." The result was a rush of joy grown rare in the recent life of the Republic. . . . At the news from Teheran, the mother of hostage Bruce German ran out into Main Street in Edwardsville, Pa., clanging a cowbell and whooping, "My Bruce is free! My Bruce is free!" She might have been a town crier ringing in an unproclaimed national holiday. Champagne and tears ran free in hostage homes. New York City proposed a ticker-tape parade of welcome. Los Angeles rekindled its Olympic

162

flame. Chicago loosed 10,000 yellow balloons over a downtown plaza. Washington finally lit its national Christmas tree, on Carter's last command as President. Bells pealed, sirens wailed and yellow ribbons fluttered everywhere. . . .[1]

The abduction of Chet merited hardly an inch in the columns of Colombian newspapers.

Brenda celebrated the hostages' return by spending most of the day at DAS headquarters repeating her story three times to various investigators. Police and government departments cross-referenced information, but the puzzle was large and the pieces in hand few.

By Wednesday, responsibility for coordinating police rescue efforts fell upon CAES (pronounced CAH-ACE), Colombia's elite Anti-Extortion and Kidnapping Command. Major Jaime Morales, head of the organization, spent long hours with Bob Whitesides gathering information and mapping strategy. Bob's quick mind and memory for details suited him well for interacting with the police on SIL's behalf.

"You're right of course," the major said, "the M-19 is our leading candidate in this affair."

"Leading, but not certain?"

"Correct."

"Who else is in the running?"

"Oh, there are any number of organizations championing the cause of the disenfranchised by tossing bombs and dumping kidnap victims into the park."

---

[1]Peter Goldman, "A Day to Remember," *Newsweek*, 2 February 1981, 18. Copyright 1981, by *Newsweek*, Inc. All Rights Reserved. Reprinted by Permission.

"Such as. . . ," Bob asked.

"Worker's Self-Defense Group, Army of National Liberation, FARC—of course, FARC is basically rural."

"Am I correct to assume, sir, the methodology in the guest-house takeover diverged from M-19's usual M.O.?"

"That's it exactly. No written demands or literature of any sort left at the site. No flags, no spray-painted revolutionary graffiti decorating the walls. Nothing."

"So we're in the dark till they contact us."

"Yes." The major leaned back in his chair. "Now about Al Wheeler. The bodyguards could use a detailed description of his schedule, his routine."

"That should be no problem."

"Also, we would advise SIL to supply a second. car—rented, or your own—to follow Wheeler's car. It's best to have one of our men in a separate vehicle."

Bob nodded.

The major hesitated. "I'm sorry we can't supply it ourselves. Most people have no idea of the drain on our department."

"Just how many extortion-kidnap cases do you get?" asked Bob.

"Counting threats? Four a week."

Bob, gave a low whistle.

"You can see, Senor Whitesides, why you're not front page news yet." Major Morales tapped his fingers on the desk. "Well," he straightened, "if you'll get me that list of, previous employees I asked for this morning, my men will get to work on it."

They stood and shook hands.

Meanwhile, the people at Lomalinda set aside a day for a different kind of work. Offices sat empty and printing presses fell silent. In place of the low hum of computers, the low murmur of voices could be heard all over the center. Mechanics and linguists, pilots and scholars, parents, teenagers, and children—together they sat in circles or knelt by their sofas and prayed for Chet and his family. They prayed for themselves, too, for God to make them wise in knowing what to do.

Will Kindberg and Joan Gardner could not stay for the day of prayer. They had a flight to catch. Since Chet's capture, Joan had been anxious to join Brenda, her daughter, in Bogota and help with the grandchildren. Will, as branch director, needed to be there to assist Brenda and direct SIL's response to the kidnapping.

The plane landed in the capital city and a taxi sped to the guest house. After visiting Brenda, Will excused himself and phoned Al Wheeler and Bob Whitesides for a status report. He then placed a call to Wycliffe's international headquarters in California to speak with the head of the Latin American division.

"I want to make sure I'm straight on our policy for hostage situations," he said. He was straight. He drove to the office of Dr. Benjamin Lopez, legal advisor to the president of Colombia. What was his government's stance toward SIL in this affair?

"We want you to stay," the official assured him.

"Our policy is not to give in to terrorists." By dinner, the tired American was meeting around a table with Colombian friends of SIL, discussing strategy and getting a feel for general public reaction. At nine-thirty, exhausted, he returned to the guest house and fell into a chair with his note pad. He had scribbled ideas for an hour when Al Wheeler called. "Yes, I understand. Thank you." He hung up the phone and sat with his forehead in his hand. "Please, run upstairs and get Joan," he asked one of the ladies. "But don't awaken Brenda."

Will and Joan talked in the living room for several minutes. How could they best break the news to Brenda? Finally Joan went for her. Brenda came down, wrapped in a robe, rubbing her eyes. "What is it? What's happened?" She was rapidly awakening.

Will glanced at Joan, then at Brenda, his face solemn.

"We have the demands," he said.

The Demands of
M-19

Carol Keels stood under the pavilion that served as the Lomalinda airport, eyes focused on her husband's plane just in from Bogota. The propellers had not yet quieted when Jack climbed from the craft and started briskly across the grass. Tension etched his face. A kidnapping complicated the life of an executive committee member. The couple met with a longer-than-usual embrace. Jack held Carol at arm's length and studied her face. "Have you heard the demands?"

"Yes."

"Well, there's really no decision to make. There's only one thing to do."

Carol nodded. "Only one thing."

Jack glanced at his watch. "I have to run, honey. We have a special EC meeting." He kissed her and mounted the back seat of a friend's Honda. The two men scooted off, and Carol returned home.

Two hours later the members of the executive committee closed their folders. "Then it's set, gentlemen," said the chairman, pleased at the unanimous agreement of the spirited debaters before him. "We're staying."

At her home across the center, Carol Keels stared at each solemn face around her lunch table. "Yes, the decision's as good as made," she told the children. "We're leaving."

So went the responses in many SIL homes to the kidnappers' demands that were publicly released just that morning—Friday, January 23, four days after Chet's abduction. Excerpts from a four-page document appeared on the front page of major Colombian newspapers. The authors identified themselves as an "urban military column" of the April 19 Movement. Included was a letter addressed to President Ronald Reagan.

"Mr. Chester Allen Bitterman, member of Wycliffe Bible Translators, is in our power," the document read. Carol mulled over the words, thinking of Chet, thinking of Brenda.

She eyed her daughters. "If we had to leave quickly and could each take only two things, what would you take?"

"He will remain our prisoner until you, Mr. President, and your government, remove from our homeland the above-mentioned company and all of its members." And they had come to help, Carol thought.

Eight-year-old Joy thought she would take her Bible. But no, that was silly. She could easily get a new one in the States.

"Our organization, the April 19 Movement (M19), has investigated the Wycliffe Bible Translators organization and has come to the conclusion . . ."

Joy loved her turtles. Such a cute family. ". . . that the above-mentioned company is an affront to the indigenous communities and to our national sovereignty."

Four turtles, Which should she take? The parents or the babies?

"Being conscious of the necessity of fighting for the national liberation and being conscious of the support given us by the indigenous communities . . ."

"I'll take my mommy and daddy turtle." The youngsters would somehow make do.

". . . the rural population, the workers, employees, students, intellectuals. . ."

Silence.

" . . . and all Colombians who are victims of imperialistic politics . . . "

Sniffles.

". . . [and so forth, and so on]"

"I'll take my braid and monkey." Twelve-year-old Kerry had decided: her flute would have to stay. Lorrie, eleven, squirmed. Her sister Kerry loved that flute. Lorrie herself loved a certain photo album.

"Mr. Bitterman's life depends on you, Mr. President, and on the government over which you preside. In order to obtain Mr. Chester Allen Bitterman's liberty, the following two conditions must be met: 1) The removal from Colombia of the organization known as Wycliffe Bible Translators, Inc. . . . 2) The publication of the document that will reach you through your ambassador in Colombia on January 25, 1981 in the Washington Post and the New York Times, as well as in European and Latin American dailies."

Lorrie decided she would take her album and. . . .

"Wycliffe Bible Translators, its linguists, and administrative personnel must leave the country. . . "

. . . her album and . . .

". . . by 6:00 P.M. on February 19, 1981, leaving behind their possessions."

. . . and Kerry's flute.

"The indigenous communities of Colombia, together with Colombian professionals in anthropology and sociology, will name a commission that will take charge of the equipment."

"And you, Janie? What about you?" Seven-year-old Janie did not blink an eye. "I'll take Joy's two turtle children!" she smiled. Her mother laughed through her tears.

(signed) National Coordinating Command of
M-19
WIN or DIE

* * *

The Colombian government reacted quickly. Hours after the printing of the terrorist demands, Government Minister German Zea Hernandez appeared on national television and radio. "The United States," said the minister, "is in no way responsible for the Summer Institute of Linguistics. It is a private organization under contract with the Colombian government. Therefore, it is with the Colombian government that the M-19 needs to negotiate. However, the national government will never negotiate under pressure."

Equally unyielding was the United States. Embassy spokesman Al Laun outlined the Reagan administration's position. "M-19 is urging the U.S. government to get the Institute out, but it is not in our power to do so." The president, Laun said, had no right to regulate the movements of American citizens abroad who were not government employees. Nor could he order the publication of articles in the free press. The safety of Mr.

Bitterman was the responsibility of the Colombian government, and therefore the U.S. would under no circumstances bargain with the terrorists. With the Colombian and American stances firm, the weight of responsibility fell upon SIL. The possibility remained that CAES would locate and rescue Chet. But short of that, the alternatives were clear: either SIL left the country, or Chet would die.

Will Kindberg winced at the thought. SIL, at its international conference in 1979, had voted into policy its long-practiced refusal to pay ransom, extortion, or blackmail of any kind. The logic was simple. First, it was morally wrong to finance subversion. Second, it was unwise. Blink first in a showdown and the word would spread. Missionaries worldwide would be jeopardized.

The logic of the policy somehow lost its luster the evening Will sat up with Brenda explaining the terrorist demands and SIL's unbending response. "That was the hardest night of my life," he would later say. "It would've been easier to tell Brenda her husband had been crushed by a truck."

Knowing where the Institute's hard-line policy could lead, Will announced that anyone in the branch was free to leave—no questions asked. Reactions ran the gamut.

"Oh no, Lord. Pete's going to want to go home." Marcia Manier found herself reliving the year and a half it had taken her and her husband to raise sufficient funds to come to Colombia. "We're going home, Marcia." Pete Manier found himself reliving the hour and a half he had spent under the gaze of a loaded revolver.

"Bang! Bang! You come with me!" Children

played "Chet Bitterman versus the terrorists." Off came the cowboy hats, on went the ski masks. Small children, too young to understand, knew only from their parents' hushed tones that a guerrilla was something awful—something you'd meet in a nightmare.

People wondered. Was it worth subjecting the children to such pressure in order to stay? Did God want SIL to leave? What would Chet say if he were asked? Had the branch considered all the options? Could SIL uproot, training Colombians to come in to take over the work? The idea had been tried, but had it been tried long enough? Hard enough? Some were uncomfortable with "sacrificing a man for the work." "I'm willing to give my life," the argument went, "but can I risk someone else's?"

Those who decided no packed their bags. The majority stayed, including Pete and Marcia. Criticism did not separate the two groups. Rather, prayer united them. Since the day Chet disappeared, Lomalinda had mobilized itself into a relentless praying force. Families and individuals signed up to intercede for their missing colleague in fifteen-minute slots around the clock. The midnight candles would burn for the next seven weeks.

* * *

Depressed. There was simply no other word to describe Mr. Bitterman's reaction to the news of his son's kidnapping . . . except maybe angry. Or shocked. Horrified. Enraged. Overwhelmed with frustration. He could tear a telephone book in half.

You couldn't tell it. Chester Allen Bitterman II did not wear his emotions on his sleeve. When his wife entered their basement office, she had questioned him concerning the scribble on his pad: "Radio message . . . guest house in Bogota broken into . . . radio equipment taken . . . Chet hostage." What was this?

Her husband continued his business conversation with the office manager. "Yes," he managed to squeeze in a sentence to Mary, "I want to talk to you about this," and finished his conversation. Only then did he usher her upstairs to discuss the call that had come from Wycliffe headquarters in California.

Jaw and eyes set, the lion prowled his house the rest of the day. He would not take this lying down. He had spent his life changing what didn't suit him. This was no exception. He would first call back Wycliffe and learn the details, all of them. Armed with this information he would set about to remedy this unfortunate mistake. He would find Chet and set him free. He would get a boat load of guns and men and go down there and . . . . The muscular scale man sat on the bed and stifled an urge to cry. Pillows crumpled in his fists.

The lion was in a cage.

An hour passed. He paced and thought and schemed. What could he do?

Mary amazed him. For a fleeting moment he had seen her lose her composure when he had explained the situation. Then she got hold of herself and prayed. "Lord, 1 don't understand this. However we look at it, it's a bad situation. But Chet's yours—we gave him to you a long time ago and we want you to take this situation and bring honor to your name." She was crazy. And right, of course.

I'll be—! No way would he ever bend to God like that! He would *do* something. What?

Another hour passed.

In the kitchen. Pouring glasses of water he didn't want. No way. No way! What could he do?

Another hour.

In the bathroom. What could he do? No way would he grovel.

Another hour.

In the basement. No way. No way. He would not get humbly on his knees and kiss the feet of whatever Providence had slept on the job while his boy got dragged off by some revolutionary scum. Pacing. Pouring. Prowling. Planning. Praying in disgust. Praying for vengeance. Praying in hate. No way would he bend. He would die first. He would die rescuing his son. What would he do? What could he do?

He stormed the beach with his men and his guns.

He crept through the jungles. He slithered down alleyways—throwing grenades, shooting radicals, busting heads, freeing Chet. He would fight. Yes, fight! No way would he bend.

In everything give thanks, for this is the will of God for you.

The Scripture verse, memorized years ago, came to him uninvited. What a stupid verse. St. Paul obviously never had a hostage son. Nothing doing. The only thanks he would ever give was over the grave of those terrorists.

In everything give thanks.

In the downstairs office. No way. Being a Christian was one thing. Licking boots like a squeamish fool was another. Give thanks—the absurd suggestion.

In the back yard. No way. Crushing skulls, yes. Tossing bombs, oh yes, yes. But getting on his knees and lying about how happy he was that those slime-born vermin had crawled out of the sewer and laid their stinking fingers on his boy? A thousand times no way! He would sail past the U.S. patrols, past the Colombian patrols, sneak in the men and guns, find his son in that city of four million people. He would storm the house, blow it to bits and kill the slime—all without a scratch to his boy. Then they would sprout wings and fly out of there. No way would he bend. No way! He would. . . . God! God! God! The desperate man dropped to his knees on the bedroom floor and sobbed like an infant, clutching the throw rug.

He would never see his boy again.

In everything give thanks.

For what! His thoughts snapped.

In everything . . .

It's not appropriate.

In everything . . .

Can't you suggest something better?

In . . .

I know. He paused. In everything. He sat a long time and held his face in his, hands. Suppose I did give thanks. What in the world, (God, I hate this) . . . what in the world could I be thankful for? I don't know how to be thankful. I'm new at this. He continued to mull over the Scriptures buried in his mind.

I'll make a list. (Pure act of the will.) Let me think. (Eyes closed. Sweating.) God promises to care for his own. I suppose I could give thanks for that. "Thank you God that you promise to care for your own." (Pause.) "You're sure as heck not doing, a very good . . . !" He caught himself. "Thank you that you promise to care for your own."

The taste of boots. What else? Well, God is big enough to keep his promises. Another swallow. "Thank you for being big enough to back up your promises."

Anything more to give praise for, rationally? The

thoughts came slowly, but they came. Chet knows and loves you. Chet has a good mind and body. If anybody could take care of himself, he could. Chet's good in Spanish and can communicate well with his captors.

Ever so gradually, a fading of the taste of boots.

Ever so gradually, a spreading of Mary's craziness, the first inklings of thankful emotions. The hours passed. The lion, pacing less, thought again of weapons. Spiritual weapons. *For the weapons we use are not those the world uses,* the verses came from somewhere in the recesses of his memory, *but divinely powerful for the pulling down of strongholds.* What are these weapons? Prayer. At least one of them is prayer. God . . . sovereign God. . . . I have a request to make. . . .

He thought. If it was good for him to pray, it was twice as good for two. Three times better for three to pray. Whom could he ask? Family, of course. And friends, friends at church. And Christian organizations—radio stations and mission boards that his family had supported over the years. These groups had hundreds, even thousands, of constituents. He had helped them over the years. Maybe they could help him.

"Hello?" The phone connection was good.

"Back to the Bible Broadcast? My wife and I have prayed for you and given to you over the years. Now, we have something we'd like you to pray for. . . . " Africa Inland Mission, WDAC Radio Station, Bible Club Movement, Unevangelized Fields Mission, Sandy Cove Bible Conference Grounds—on into the day he called. At 5:00 P.M. he and Curt had to leave for an overnight job in Maryland. Mary and his daughter Connie continued the calls into the early morning hours. Lancaster Day Christian School, Columbia Bible College, relatives in Arizona, friends in Alaska.

The organizations had constituents, and the constituents had friends, and the friends had churches, and the churches had members, and many had radio and TV shows, and newsletters, and the newspapers came, and the TV stations came, and by the end of the week prayer was ascending for Chet in Spanish, Swedish, German, Hindi, Japanese, Russian, and a score of tribal languages that the Bittermans could scarcely pronounce.

The Keeper had unlocked the cage.

In the Public Arena

January 30, 1981, Huntington Beach, California

For several hours the protesters had sat on their cars and stood about on the sidewalk. Now the media arrived and they began to march. Their posters were not subtle.

WYCLIFFE MURDERS

CULTURE DESTROYERS

REMEMBER THE MASSACRE

Through parted blinds in Wycliffe's U.S. Division headquarters, director Bernie May watched the demonstrators parade along Beach Boulevard. College homework had changed over the years, he grimaced. University of California at Irvine, Social Science 198E, "Community Organizing Practicum." As a courtesy the *Los Angeles Times* had forwarded to him yesterday's press release from the student group stating its intent to picket.

Bernie later learned that the professor had no prior knowledge of the march. For now, that didn't matter. Nor did it matter that the students numbered only 15 of UCI's 10,000 enrolled. What mattered was that the lies and confusion Wycliffe routinely faced overseas had now reached home.

To America.

"What are you going to do, Bern?" An associate broke in to the director's thoughts. "Invite them in for coffee?"

The idea had crossed his mind. But this crowd looked angry. It might turn ugly. Some of the staff talked about working late to avoid the walk to their cars.

"I'm going to accept that interview with Channel 7."

"Now?"

"Yes. "

"What if they distort your points? You know what TV editing can do."

"Yes, but what do we imply if we say nothing?"

"They'll hit you with the Guahibo incident."

Bernie knew. In 1970 violence had erupted in Colombia between Guahibo Indians and white settlers who were encroaching upon their land. The government requested Wycliffe linguists to act as translators for investigating soldiers. When the facts became clear the government sided with the Guahibos and defended their territory. But the story spread that Wycliffe had provided air and radio support to government troops as they stamped out a Guahibo insurrection against the land-hungry white settlers. Anthropological and religious groups worldwide had believed the story.

"You ready?"

Bernie nodded. They could lose nothing by telling the truth. He turned and started down the hall toward the lobby. Jesus had said to expect misunderstanding. "If they persecuted me, they will persecute you. . . . They will treat you this way because of my name."

He didn't mind. A march was just that—nothing more. But he felt for Brenda. What would she think of this?

* * *

The rustle of sheets broke the silence. Then came a groan, a deep one, the sort that makes an onlooker feel helpless. Chet Bitterman doubled in pain from a gall-bladder attack. Sweat from his body soaked the sheets.

"Chet?"

Brenda sat up and reached beside her. The sheets were dry and cool.

She caught her breath and brushed the hair from her eyes. Two A.M., read the clock. Every night she did this, about the time Chet would have his attacks.

Across the room Esther stirred from a fitful sleep, waking Anna Ruth with her whimpering. Brenda carried them to her own bed. Bad dreams had been a problem ever since Chet had vanished two weeks ago.

Two weeks. He must be wearing down; she was. How long could a person go on praying and fasting and hoping? Surely Chet would be home any day. His packed suitcase lay by her feet.

Esther had fallen back to sleep but Anna's eyes lit the room. "Mama, I don't want papa tied up in those bad men's house. I want him to come home." Brenda rocked the girls. Was Chet awake? Was he even alive? She couldn't tell from the photos the kidnappers had sent to the papers. In them, three hooded terrorists stood guard over a puffy-faced prisoner who vaguely resembled Chet. The man sat at a table staring ahead blankly. Was it him? His face looked swollen. He wore a white pullover she did not recognize, and no moustache. She had never seen him without a moustache. The signature at the bottom of the pictures looked real.

"Anna Ruth, let's pray for papa to remember his verses." They prayed. Brenda thought about the books of the Bible that Chet had memorized: James, Philippians, most of 1 Peter, a dozen or more psalms. Some of the books and passages she had learned with him.

> St. Paul from a Roman prison, Philippians 1:12-14—Now I want you to know, brothers, that what has happened to me has served to advance the gospel. As a result, it has become clear throughout the whole palace guard and to everyone else that I am in chains for Christ. Because of my chains, most of the brothers in the Lord have been encouraged to speak the word of God more courageously and fearlessly.

That should lighten his heart. God, help him recall it.

Anna tapped Brenda's arm. "God is bigger than those bad men," she said. Her simple statement of truth took Brenda aback. Truth seemed dim lately. The police were dry on clues. Cuba had come out publicly in favor of the kidnapping. Worse yet, Jaime Bateman had published his strange article in the papers yesterday. Bateman, the still-at-large leader of M-19, denied that his organization held Chet. Some splinter group, he charged, had plagiarized the M-19 name. The pretenders should come out of the-closet and dialogue—only then could the revolutionary forces be united and save the country from militarism and injustice.

Oh sure, thought Brenda. What kind of trick was

this? Her mind seesawed between confusion and fear. She was afraid of what they might do to Chet (whoever they were). Afraid of using the phones (they might be bugged). Afraid of having her picture in the papers (she might be recognized). Afraid of running into one of the terrorists in a store or parking lot. What if a familiar pair of eyes suddenly met hers? The thought gave her chills. Fear, she knew, had sent her plowing into Will the night of the terrorist demands. Didn't he care about Chet? He was branch director. He was the one M-19 really wanted. She told him so. Now she felt awful about it.

Her one comfort was the Scriptures. Yesterday she came across Isaiah 43:4. "Since you are precious in my sight and I love you, I will give other men in your place and other peoples in exchange for your life." God had originally spoken the words through Isaiah the prophet to the people of Israel who were facing military defeat and exile. Did the promise apply to Chet as well? She hoped so. She thought so. Yes, she was certain. God was, speaking to her, telling her that Chet would be freed. She would claim the promise as her own. Thank you, God.

"Mama?"

The rocking had not lured Anna Ruth back to sleep.

"Mama, when papa comes home maybe he'll let me lie next to him."

Brenda buried her face in her daughter's hair. Yes, sweetie.

* * *

Heavy breaths sounded in tandem with the swish of running shoes as Will Kindberg entered the second mile of his evening neighborhood run. The mountains, only two miles distant, were all but invisible by now. Falling dusk had coaxed on vehicle headlights.

The damp air felt good in contrast to the stifling tension of the guest house. All that jumping like mousetraps at the ring of a phone or doorbell had put him on edge. Even the meter reader had caused a stir. Tomorrow he would search for other quarters.

Through the dimness he glimpsed two male shapes on the sidewalk a half block away. He kept to the street until they had passed, then trotted back up on the curb. He did not look behind.

Why, he wondered, was he not usually afraid? Others were afraid. He had felt it last week in the auditorium at Lomalinda where he briefed everyone on the terrorist demands. He saw it in Brenda's eyes when she first learned of the ultimatum.

Perhaps he was too busy to be afraid. He spent his time trying to help Chet and the family. And then there were holes in the dike to be plugged: branch morale, branch unity, doubts about policy . . .

. . . .public relations.

El Bogotano, Sat., Jan. 31, 1981
"SIL Deceives Indian Population"

A commission from members of the Cholos Indian community has asked the governor of Cauca [a state ,in southwest Colombia] to evict several North Americans who want to install a branch of the Summer Institute of Linguistics in the region . . . . The Institute has been a front page news item in recent days due to the kidnapping of Chester A. Bitterman. . . . The Institute has entered many countries under the pretext of "literacy" among Indian groups, and has been dedicated to ruining the culture of native Indians, teaching them strange beliefs and, what is worse, taking their lands. . . . Indian leaders said that the "linguists" plan to bring machinery into the area and to exploit the region's gold deposits.

Same song second verse, thought Will. Wycliffe had come to expect such treatment from *El Bogotano*—considered by many the most radical and sensationalist of the city's daily papers. For years it had led the pack in anti-SIL name calling and mud slinging. Still, the timing of the article hurt.

He rounded a corner and almost collided with two children. "Ho, Perdón." He must look where he was going. His mind was on his own article in yesterday's paper. The beginning of the campaign.

The Summer Institute of Linguistics is a scientific and humanitarian organization. . . composed of Christian people who, for the love of God, have dedicated their lives to the support of humanity—especially to the indigenous communities that lack a written language....

Al Wheeler, Bob Whitesides, and he had wrestled long and hard about that article. Rarely, if ever, had Wycliffe defended itself in the press of a host country. Jesus had told his disciples to love their enemies and turn the other cheek.

True, countered Bob. But did that mean saying nothing? Had not St. Paul appealed his case to Caesar and given passionate speeches in defense of

Christianity before Roman authorities? A Wycliffe response in the newspapers would not stem from personal vindictiveness but from a desire to uphold the truth and free Chet. The terrorist ploy to discredit the Institute must not go unchallenged. Colombian advisers to SIL agreed. The press had been neutral, at best, toward Wycliffe during the Bitterman affair. Public opinion was being manipulated.

"We have a saying in Colombia for people who refuse to answer their accusers," said one adviser.

"Oh?"

"Silence proves guilt."

The words hit their mark. The campaign for Chet's life had begun.

First came the SIL communique. Then, additional artillery. Radio stations read letters from Lomalinda school children on "What I Liked About Chet Bitterman." Claudette Garcia-Peña, a spirited business manager and Colombian friend of SIL, marched into the office of one of the editors of the newspaper *El Tiempo* and dropped a stack of articles on his desk.

"These are *EI Tiempo* clippings from the past six years that slander SIL with a vengeance." Her eyes left no doubt as to her mood. "Nonsense like this set the stage for M-19 to kidnap Bitterman and then think the world would applaud. You're as much to blame for his disappearance as anybody. What are you going to do about it?"

The gun barrel smoked.

Immediately *El Tiempo*'s tone softened. Within a week it issued an editorial calling for Chet's release and squarely placing blame for any forthcoming violence on M-19. With the highly respected *El*

Tiempo going out on a limb for a foreigner, other papers followed suit. Reporters flew to Lomalinda, asking how they could help. Coverage became positive. Chet Bitterman began an evolution in Colombian minds and newspapers. The once-mysterious gringo now had a wife and hometown. The alleged CIA man possessed wit and an enviable soccer dribble. He loved children. You would want him for a neighbor.

Al Wheeler and Bob Whitesides began to receive understanding looks as they passed through the Ministry lobby. Cafe chatter sympathized with the North American who had come to help the Indians. In a rare gesture Protestant and Catholic leaders joined supporting hands in the press. From the Colombian Institute of Anthropology came a most unexpected telegram of sympathy.

Yet for all this, it was a letter from Chet, received by Brenda exactly two weeks after the kidnapping and published the following day, which did more good than SIL's entire media campaign.

> 24 January 1981
> My Dearest Brenda:
> I am fine. As unnatural as it may seem, please do not—or at least try not to—worry for/about me. I have not experienced any physical hardships to present—including gall-bladder attacks.

Brenda studied the handwritten pages hungrily. At least he was alive! His handwriting seemed normal. His wrists must not be tied.

> The hardest thing for me so far has been thinking about how you are handling all this. It would help me more than anything to

know that you are holding strong. The girls will cue their reactions off you. Remember what Ken Williams said. The situation is not what causes stress. It is our perception of the situation that causes stress.

The Lord brought 2 Corinthians 2:14 (I think that's it, mas o menos) to mind: "But thanks be to God, who always leads us in triumph through the Lord Jesus Christ." The word for "triumph" was used for the Roman victory parades, when the soldiers were received back at home by the cheering crowds after a successful battle. That verse was Dr. McQuilkin's[1] life verse. I have had a lot of free time ☺ to think about such things as Daniel's 3 friends (by the way, they are supposed to be bringing me a Bible— Spanish—this afternoon) and Paul and Silas' experience in the jail at Philippi.

In the case of Daniel's friends, God did something very unusual through His power for a specific purpose—so that through everything, all concerned would learn (i.e., have their misconceptions corrected) about Him. The result of the experience was that everyone learned who He was. Remember Paul and the Praetorian Guard. Keep this in your thoughts for me. Wouldn't it be neat if something special like this would happen? Then we can get on with the Carijonas.

"Therefore, since Christ also suffered in His body, arm yourselves with the same attitude, because he who has suffered in his body is done with sin. As a result, he does not live the rest of his earthly life for evil human desires, but rather, for the will of God." 1 Peter 4: 1-2

---

[1] Founder of Columbia Bible College

> I am also studying and learning a lot about Marxism. Tell Mother and Father that Master/Visa needs some immediate attention.
>
> All my love—to the girls too—Chet

Brenda sat, stood, then sat again. She bit her lip and smiled. He *had* remembered his verses. The joy within her spread like the warmth of good soup on a cold day. She set the letter down. A postscript she had not noticed on the back page caught her eye.

> P.S. Brenda: I have to tell you that it is very important that you collaborate with my captors and that you all should leave Colombia.

This was not Chet. He was being forced. She read the words again.

> P.S. Brenda: I have to tell you that it is very important that you collaborate with my cap*lie*tors and that you all should *lie*ve Colombia.

She smiled. It was Chet, all right.

The postscript was not published in order to protect Chet from reprisals.

In response to Wycliffe, Chet's abductors stepped up their own press campaign.

Carlos Tello worked alone at his desk in the early evening hours of February 9, 1981. From the sixth-floor office of the Inter-Press Service, a Rome-based news agency, he could hear the traffic of the Bogota streets below.

The door buzzer rang. Threading his way past empty desks and abandoned work stations he answered the door. Two men and two women, well-dressed, wished to interview the agency's director. Why four people were needed for one interview Mr. Tello was not certain. In any case, the director was not in. They would have to return tomorrow.

The group produced pistols and a hand grenade. Mr. Tello swallowed. They were certainly welcome to come in.

At gunpoint Mr. Tello cabled a ten-line message: Chester Allen Bitterman was in the hands of the National Coordinating Command of M-19 and his freedom could be had only if the Summer Institute of Linguistics left the country. The Institute was in violation of Colombia's national sovereignty and acted as a Trojan horse for the United States Army and American corporations such as Exxon. Its bases trained Colombian army troops in repressive techniques and were served by vertical takeoff aircraft.

Mr. Tello was then shown to the bathroom and told that dynamite would blow him to bits if he tried to leave. The visitors spray-painted the walls with "M-19, Win or Die" and went home.

Mr. Tello left the bathroom and canceled the transmission.

That same day, the M-19 high command issued a second press statement denying that they had Chet.

All that week stickers appeared on walls and in telephone booths around the capital city:

> In the past, the commoners against the Spanish. Today, the people of (South) America against Yankee imperialism. SIL: Get out! (signed) M-19

But the terrorist campaign did not end with words.

"Al, will you look at this?"

His raincoat damp, Al Wheeler joined Bob Whitesides and several F-2 officials in the bare fluorescent-lit room. The men stood examining two lead pipes laid out on a table, each an inch and a half in diameter and about a foot long. Al studied the pipes.

"Black powder and sugar," an F-2 man volunteered. "Plugged at the ends with these materials."

Al pursed his lips. "How much damage could they have done?"

"To structures? Minimal. To be frank, pipe bombs are designed for human targets." The official awaited a facial response that did not come.

"The fuses are here."

Al fingered the strands and eyed Bob.

"Wet," he said. He glanced at the F-2 official. "I thought fuses were waterproof."

"They can be."

"Why do you suppose these weren't?"

"Hard to say. An oversight, a—"

"Warning." Bob interrupted.

The official shrugged. "Could be that, too."

Al squinted at the deadly components. "Celia and the others are all right?"

Bob nodded. "A little shaken, that's all. Like we said, the explosives didn't blow at either house."

Al stared out the window. Celia Olivera was an unabashed friend of the Institute who rented space in her three-story townhouse to two single Wycliffe ladies and a translator couple. He could understand her home being attacked. But the old guest house?

"We haven't used the La Soledad location for . . . what's it been? Two years?"

Bob nodded again.

"That means they're going on two-year-old information. What do we make of that?"

The F-2 man answered. "It's a point in favor of the National Coordinating Command being a splinter group. Maybe Bateman's right. Maybe M-19 doesn't have Chet. They're generally too professional to make such big mistakes."

Indeed, there was mounting evidence that an M-19 breakaway group existed. No characteristic spray-painting or literature had been left in the guest house on the day of the kidnapping. When literature did arrive, it espoused Marxist doctrine in addition to the usual, purely nationalistic line. Operations displayed a certain amateurishness— the abductors had assumed Al Wheeler to be head of the Colombian Branch (which he was not) and the old guest house to be still in use.

Hostages interviewed after the Dominican Embassy affair had reported discussions among the terrorists that showed an ideological division. Some wanted violence. Others favored surfacing, accepting a government offer of amnesty, and entering the political arena.

Still, it was possible that M-19 had taken Chet but then voiced a denial when their plan backfired and public reaction shifted. SIL could not be sure whom it was dealing with. The confusion added to Brenda's malaise. "My feelings go from being encouraged that the Lord will bring Chet home alive," she wrote in her diary, "to wondering if Chet will ever come back. What a lack of faith I have, and yet I want to be realistic." The thought of her girls affected Brenda most. "I need someone big and strong," said Anna Ruth. "I need Papa. We need to write him a thank-you note so he'll come home."

"John 3:16," he said, "I'll huff and puff and have everlasting life." (Chet, age 4 pictured at right) "He finished the last end-of-the-chapter question then signed the paper 'Abraham Lincoln' as usual."

(Chet's 5th and 6th grade class at Lancaster Christian Day School; Chet at far right, Beth Van Ormer behind him)

"But his pranks, that crew cut, and those diddly bops . . ." (6th grade)

"Everyone soon learned that Bitterman loved to wrestle." (Chet pictured above, front row on left) "Leaning back from the mirror on slender hips . . . . satisfying himself that every wave was in place." (1970), high school senior year

"... laughing, talking, looking very much at home with each other." (Chet with Beth Van Ormer, Christmas, 1970) "And he never condemned me," Tim said of Chet years later. (At Columbia Bible College with one of his "surrogate mothers," Marlita, and friend Tim Thompson)

"He was interested in everybody...." (With Ica Indians who visited Lomalinda; photography by Brenda Bitterman Jackson)

Chet is seen here with daughter Anna Ruth in Costa Rica, taking a break from language study. (Photography by Brenda Bitterman Jackson) The second photograph was taken six months after the Bittermans' arrival at Lomalinda. Anna Ruth is 2 1/2; Esther is several weeks old." They would spend their lives in Colombia—their place was with the Indians." (Photography by George Gardner, Brenda's father)

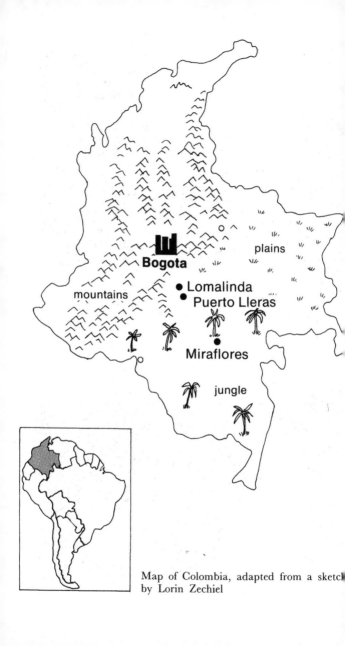

Map of Colombia, adapted from a sketch by Lorin Zechiel

"It was Chet's manner to play the right forward wing." (Playing the soldiers at Lomalinda; photography by George Gardner) Puerto Lleras, or "Port"—the small town four miles from Lomalinda where the guerrilla informant shot himself. (Photography courtesy of SIL Colombia)

Lomalinda's airport pictured above. Below, the SIL guest house in Bogota." Nothing about the white, two-story townhouse stood out from the rest of the street." (Photography by George Gardner)

The city of Bogota, ". . . hugging the mountain base, four million strong." (Courtesy of *El Tiempo*)

At right is the Ministry of Government building (center building, far side of street) with SIL offices on the seventh and eighth floors. Chet drove here daily from the guest house while living in Bogota." The drive downtown takes forty-five minutes under normal conditions. Of course, I've never seen conditions norma!." (Both courtesy of SIL Colombia)

Graffiti on a Bogota building: "Bolivar, your sword will continue in battle until the final victory. M-19." (M-19 stole the historic sword from the Bolivar Museum in January, 1974. It is now used to induct members into Colombia's guerrilla movement. Courtesy of SIL Colombia)

"His face looked swollen. He wore a white pullover she did not recognize and had no moustache. She had never seen him without a moustache." (This was the first photo released by the guerrillas. Photography from UPI/Bittertmann Newsphotos; used by permission)

There was Chet, as big as life, in the papers. Grinning. Playing chess. (Courtesy of *El Bogotano*)

"But Chet's not the first person to have died for me." (Al Wheeler—M-19 had intended to kidnap him. Courtesy of SIL Columbia)

"Bob took the receiver, prepared not to do business. . . ." (Bob Whitesides, above, at the second press conference, hours before Chet's murder.)" . . . getting a feel for general public reaction." (Will Kindberg, Colombian branch director at the time of the kidnapping. Photography by Bea Messa)

"Three hooded terrorists stood guard over a puffy-faced prisoner who vaguely resembled Chet. The man sat at a table staring ahead blankly." (Courtesy of *El Tiempo*)

"Police found his body in the bus where he died , in a parking lot in the south of town." (Courtesy of *El Espectador*)

". . . he's kicked the ball to us." (Front right, Tom Branks; center, Rev. Abadia, the Bittermans' Colombian pastor; courtesy of George DeVoucalla) Memorial service on March 29, 1981, at Calvary Independent, Chet's home church in Lancaster, Pennsylvania. Front row: Brenda, George and Joan Gardner, David and Glenn Gardner (Brenda's brothers), Becky Gardner (David's wife), Mary and Chet Bitterman, Curt Bitterman with wife Diane. Second row: Connie, Carol, Craig (with wife Dawn), Grant, Chris, and Cindy. (From Richard Hertzler, *Lancaster New Era*)

"That man is Jesus.. . . . My daddy's with him now," (Courtesy of Richard Hertzler, *Lancaster New Era*)

Kidnapped missionary writes that he's unharmed

A letter handwritten by Chester Bitterman 3d, the Lancaster missionary-linguist who was kidnapped by guerrillas in Bogota, Colombia, on Jan. 19, was delivered to a newspaper in Bogota and then forwarded to his

Guerrillas Postpone Execution Deadline

BOGOTA, Colombia (UPI) — Leftist guerrillas let the deadline for executing American translator Chester B— him, but reports

their languages and translate Bible into those languages. T— have two young daughters.

Bitterman, 28, was kidnapped institute's residence in Bogota al days before he was sched—have a gall bladder operation.

Guerrillas in Colombia blame CIA

Worshippers Pray For Bitterman's Life

March 5 New Bitterman Death Date

AY EVENING, MARCH 3, 1981   Price 20¢ — Daily Home Delivered $1.20 A Week

'Mystery' Telephone Call

Bitterman Reported Dead by Guerrilla But US Doesn't Believe It

By ED KLIMUSKA
New Era Staff Writer

In another dramatic and confusing development in the Colombia kidnapping of missionary Chester A. Bitterman III, an apparent spokesman for his guerrilla captors hinted Monday that the Lancaster County native has been killed.

However, Bitterman's associates in the South American country continued today to believe that he was still alive.

—before noon today. Al

rillas demands and leave the country ran out more than a week ago.

• A Colombia radio network reported Bitterman was killed, but it was very cautious in its account

• Many Colombian radios are reporting that their newsmen believe Bitterman has been killed.

• One Colombian morning newspaper reported Bitterman was killed several days ago, but two others carried no accounts of his execution.

Bitterman, 28, is a linguist and Bible translator who was in Colombia 18 months before his kidnapping. His captors, believed to be a splinter — of the M-19 Movement charge — CIA front

rs at Calvary Independe—
or Chester A. Bitterman I
stage in Colombia.

—4-19, also claimed—
document delivered to foreign e—
spondents that the United S
operated a secret missile base
vast wildlife park in the inter

LANCASTER, PA., SATURDAY EVENING, MARCH 7, 1981   Price 20¢ — Daily Home Delivered $1.20

U.S. Angry, Says 'It Was Cold Blooded Murder'

Bitterman Is Executed
His Body Found in Bu

'God's Will,' Says Bitterman's Mother

Reagan offers condolences

uerrillas.
aughters have been repo
he U.S. Embassy.

M-19, one of the most a
ombia's guerrilla group
gave the institute 48
close its operations in C

It was time for another media attempt.

More communiques. More invitations for outsiders to inspect Lomalinda. And this time, an open letter from Brenda to the abductors, in Spanish, written on Valentine's Day.

> Dear Commander,
>
> With all my heart, I am writing to you hoping that I can express my desire for Chet to be set free.
>
> I want to thank you for giving Chet permission to write to me on January 24. I was very concerned for him, far more than you can imagine. It makes me and the girls feel a lot better to know that he is in good health and that you are treating him well. On the exact day he was kidnapped we had planned an outing to Sopo Park, so that Chet could spend some good time with the girls before going to the hospital for gall-bladder surgery.
>
> When you were here in the house you saw my two girls when they kissed their papa good-bye. Do you realize how much they need him? They are always asking for him and I don't know what to tell them. They remember when their papa would play with them on the floor pretending to be elephants and tigers and they would laugh and laugh. He would tell them fantastic stories and they would listen with enthusiasm. Very often they say to me, "When is Papa coming to hug or hold me?"
>
> It is true that not everyone has the fortune of having a papa, but when they have one, it is so marvelous that nothing can compare. Please don't let the children remain without a papa. Anna Ruth is only three years old and Esther Elisabeth, who was born in Colom-

bia, hardly walks. They don't understand why some men took away their papa by force. How do 1 explain this? Should I say that in Colombia they don't care?

I know that you are concerned about the future of your brothers in Colombia and therefore you fight for a better and more just world. We, although by a different method, also are fighting for a change. However, the way we do it is by loving people.

Certainly time is passing quickly and we can't stop it. Please communicate with me by whatever way you want, perhaps in our post office box. Chet knows the number.

As you are living with Chet in these days you will have the opportunity to get to know him and I am sure that you will be friends. The only thing Chet wanted in life was to be dedicated to God, his family, and a group of Colombian Indians.

His desire to communicate with the Colombians is profound. From the beginning he was dedicated to learning Spanish and you will realize this as he talks to you. With the same determination, Chet wanted to speak the Indian language where we were going to work.

I have faith in Chet's return. Behind the guns you carried there was a slight glimmer of kindness, and for this reason I have confidence in you. Remember when you said that as soon as you had the information that you needed from Chet you would bring him back?

Please return Chet! My girls and I need him so much. Don't kill him, I beg you, it will do you no good.

With all my heart I ask God to bless you and show you our anguished hearts and the necessity for Chet to be with us again.

Brenda Bitterman
Bogota
February 14, 1981

The day after Brenda wrote her letter, a Colombian radio station broadcast a Spanish tape from Chet to Brenda. It began with a statement from the guerrillas:

> The National Coordinating Command of the M-19 notifies the members of SIL that as of 18:00 hours on February 19, 1981 they should leave the country. If they do not comply, we will understand this as a challenge to nationwide violence, something that our guerrillas are ready to undertake, win or die.

> We continue with a message from Mr. Chester Allen Bitterman:

> "Good morning, Brenda. Today is February 13. How are you? Even though I know you can't answer me, I want to ask you this."

At the sound of Chet's voice, Anna Ruth squealed with delight. "Papa!" she burst out, her face aglow. "I can't wait to see you, Papa!" Brenda had to quiet her to hear the tape.

> "OK . . . I want you to know that I am very well. I am not experiencing any difficulties, at least physical ones, and I am being well cared for. The food is very good and our relationship is like a two-sided wall. On the one side is our personal relationship and on this side of the wall we have no problems at all. You could say that we are

friends. They like me and I like them and we have not had any difficulty.

"On the other side of the wall there is the ideological problem—the political point of view and we do have our differences. We understand the world in a very different way and we have had many discussions. We have discussed all this extensively. I don't know whether . . . I don't know if I have accomplished anything from all the time we have spent. We have had some very good talks.

"I hope that the girls are very well and all the . . . I forgot to say something. I want you to know I have not had any further gall-bladder attacks, at least up till now. I am very happy about that. I don't have anything further to say for now.

"Much love to the little ones and to the rest at Lomalinda. I hope they are all well. I love you very much, Brenda. Till then. . . .'"

Anna grinned from ear to ear as the tape recorder clicked off.

"Now we're not sad anymore. Today he said, 'Hello.' Tomorrow he'll say, 'I'm coming home.'"

Chet also sent a written note, repeating the taped message but adding a list of Bible references he had found helpful.

Within the same twenty-four hours as the tape broadcast, M-19 twice took to the spotlight. First, three Colombian journalists were kidnapped and forced to interview a Bateman associate and M-19 leader who claimed his organization did not have Chet. Then, M-19 guerrillas interfered with the audio portion of an evening television show. "We are not responsible for Bitterman's kidnapping," they announced. They suggested that Colombian security forces had abducted him in an effort to discredit and split up the M-19.

Back and forth. SIL in the media. M-19 in the media. Public sympathy was with SIL, but the terrorists weren't budging. There had to be more— an additional pressure, an alternative track. Wycliffe needed to talk with Chet's abductors. But how? How could they talk when they did not even know whom they were dealing with?

The how was not long in coming.

A Chain's Weakest Link

In the south of Bogota, where the buildings are low and the rent high, Elsie Veen sat in the dimness of her third-floor apartment waiting for the phone to ring. The Belgian social worker did not look her fifty-eight years. She had come to Colombia in the forties during the Violence to help the homeless and wounded. With her dark hair and skin, the slight woman could pass for Colombian. What did Martinez want? Probably someone to set up an abortion for one of his wives. He could forget it.

The phone rang. Elsie hesitated for several rings, then picked it up.

"Aló? Elsie? It's Rodolfo. I need your help."

She tried to sound confident. "Rodolfo Martinez. I heard you would call." Her words came forced. She didn't like talking to him. "What could a man of the world like you want from an old spinster like me?"

She hadn't seen him for years. She recalled Rodolfo the young man, promising and witty. It was when he had first embraced Christianity, a product of one of the American missions. He had attended one of their Bible schools and been elected a student leader; soon he was pastoring. Clever fellow. The affair had gotten him a big head. In time he had been a writer, a lawyer, a semi-legal real-estate agent. At least three foreign missions had employed him at one time or another—a shadow of scandal had always accompanied his leaving. Now he was eyeing a Senate seat.

Elsie had once been like a mother to him. But she had long since gotten disgusted with his "twisted Jacobness" as she called it. His father had been murdered for political reasons: she hoped the same would not happen to him.

"Elsie, for old time's sake, I need your help. For the sake of friendship. I want to get in touch with Al Wheeler."

Al Wheeler? What could Martinez possibly want with him? Rodolfo had once been the Institute's lawyer before his lack of credentials became known. Now he outspokenly criticized SIL's presence in the country. He knew where Al lived. Why couldn't he call him?

"Elsie, are you there?"

"I'm here. If you want him, why can't you call him?"

Martinez's breath came fast. "Because I'm certain his phones are bugged. Can I come see you? I tell you it's urgent. It has to do with Chet Bitterman."

A gasp, barely audible, escaped her. Chet Bitterman? She had not expected this.

Since 1962 when Wycliffe entered the country, Elsie had frequent occasion to brush shoulders with SIL people. Some, such as the Wheelers and Whitesides, she considered good friends. Christian expatriates tended to move in the same circles. Still, urban terrorists, telephone taps, and arranging back-room meetings were out of her league. Her conscience twitched. Hadn't she just prayed for Chet half an hour ago offering to help in any way? Maybe heaven was calling her bluff. Could she back away? She had met Chet only once, but he had impressed her. She rubbed her eyes and sighed.

"Okay, Rodolfo. Come to my apartment to-night."

Elsie pressed the receiver and dialed the White-sides'. Bob had a cool head and quick mind. He would know what to do.

"Yes, have him over. Pull his tongue. We'll be praying. "

That evening, for the first time in a long while, Elsie stared into the commanding brown eyes and oval face of her former protégé, Rodolfo Martinez. He had put on weight. Tucked under his arm was a red folder with four documents from the National Coordinating Command of M-19. In his hand was Chet's college ring. There was no doubt—he had been with the terrorists.

He began his pitch: Obviously, Martinez explained, his interest in this affair sprang from no affection for SIL. But he felt sorry for Chet and wished to save a man's life. He was willing to act as negotiator between SIL and M-19, whatever personal inconvenience it meant for him. The plan was simple: Elsie was to contact Wheeler. Martinez would expect a call from her the next day. If Wheeler agreed to a meeting she would say, "Hello, Rodolfo, it's a lovely day. Chao. Chao. Chao. Chao." If not, the message would be "Rodolfo, what a horrible day. I can't have lunch with you. Chao. Chao. Chao. Chao." The nervous Colombian confessed his fear of the police. They must not know.

The next morning before church Al Wheeler opened his door to Bob Whitesides, Will Kindberg, and Elsie.

"Elsie! What a pleasure. Frankly, I though Bob was bringing something from M-19. "

The woman smiled. "I am something from M-19. Imagine that."

They moved inside and ten minutes later Elsie had laid out the previous night's details. Martinez's unexpected offer took the men aback. Five people before him had volunteered and been rejected for the job of go-between, compromise with the terrorists on basic issues being unthinkable. Yet here had stepped forward a man known to them, however disreputable, who could prove he had *been with* Chet's captors and who said they wished to talk.

This new development, unrivaled in potential, merited special consideration. Will ventured a first opinion.

"If by negotiating we mean signaling a willingness to leave the country, then it's clear we can't negotiate. But I think there's a difference between negotiation and dialogue."

"How so?" Al's legs stretched out before him halfway under the table.

"I think Will's referring to the fact that this whole thing has backfired in M-19's face—or whoever's face," replied Bob. "They wanted publicity, but not the kind they're getting. It's possible these fellows are looking for a way to bow out without losing face."

"And they would settle for some small concession?" said Al.

"Could be."

Al nodded.

"I'm sure you gentlemen don't need any reminders of Rodolfo's reputation," interjected Elsie. "Can we trust him?"

"She's got a point," said Bob. "His credibility's low. Besides, he was the first to step forward and offer to negotiate. I think I told you what Major Morales said: nine times out of ten the first offer comes from someone tied in with the abductors."

"What option do we have?" asked Will. "As you well know, Thursday's the big day."

Indeed, that Thursday was February 19, the deadline for SIL to leave the country by 6:00 P.M. or see Chet killed. Tension mounted with each day. Even as they spoke the media war grew fierce: Brenda's open letter aired side by side with renewed terrorist threats. A pressure valve, a stall for time, was crucial. Informed friends had long advised the Institute to employ a Colombian in any dialogue with Chet's captors. Voice inflections and cultural subtleties could easily be missed by a foreigner, however fluent in Spanish.

Reluctantly, the group agreed to go with Martinez. But there would be conditions. Martinez wanted to meet at the Pozzetto Restaurant. That would not do. M-19 might be tailing him. They devised an alternate spot and agreed on Elsie as go-between, at least for the present. Carefully the group worked out her instructions.

"Is there any danger?" frowned Al Wheeler.

Eyes shifted about the table. Elsie shook her head. "I don't think so. At least not while Chet's alive." The room grew quiet. There was nothing to be said.

A knock on the door prompted Al to his. feet to peer out the window. "My bodyguard just pulled up. If Martinez is as scared as Elsie says, we'd better not let her be seen. She could lead someone to him."

They whisked her through the garage and she caught a bus home.

At 2:55 P.M. Elsie sat on a low stone wall beside the Pozzetto Restaurant. Martinez was due at 3:00. For the past half hour she had surveyed the elegant, cream brick building inside and out and seen no one suspicious. She waited.

Three young men strolling up the sidewalk slowed their pace as they neared her. She could feel their stares. Loitering about in make-up and dressy outfit, she had been misread.

"Ssssss! Insects!"

Her rebuff sent them scuttling. She chuckled. Her, a street walker—imagine that.

At two minutes after three Martinez's tan Volkswagen rounded the corner. Before he could park, Elsie was on her feet. She flagged him down and scooted into his vehicle. His seven-year-old son sat quietly in the rear.

"Rodolfo, we're not staying here. Just keep on driving."

Rodolfo drove on. Reaching beside him on the seat, he picked up the red folder from the previous night and handed it to Elsie. "You carry this. I'm dead scared of the police. In case they stop us I want you holding the papers, not me."

"Okay, Rodolfo. Is anybody tailing you?"

"No."

"Are you sure?"

"There is no one!" he insisted.

For twenty minutes Elsie directed him through the city in a senseless pattern. Her eyes wandered to the shoulder bag on the front seat. It was easily machine-gun size. She tried to control her imagination.

Finally she said, "Rodolfo, we're going to Unicentro. Turn left up here." Martinez drove to the huge shopping center, got his parking ticket, and the three walked indoors.

Elsie led him up and down hallways until satisfied that no one was following. "We're going to the bowling club," she announced. "Al Wheeler said to meet him there. Do you know where it is?"

"No. We'll have to ask at the information booth."

As they neared the cubicle, Martinez grabbed Elsie by the arm and halted. "Elsie, there's a policeman!"

"So what?"

"I don't want him to see me."

"But we've got to ask somebody."

Reluctantly, Martinez approached the booth and got his answer. He returned, sweating. "Downstairs." The trio took the escalator and found their way to the bowling club. Inside, Martinez told the others to find a chair while he studied the lanes. In a moment he reappeared, taking a seat beside Elsie, looking the other way—a man in a crowded building forced to find a chair beside a stranger.

"He's in the end alley," he breathed from the side of his mouth. "Go make contact. Tell him I'm here. And locate his gun."

"Okay, Rodolfo," she answered in kind. She assumed "his gun" meant his bodyguard.

Elsie walked the length of the bowling club to where lanky Al Wheeler was knocking down pins with precision. "Here I am, Al." He greeted her warmly, kissing her on the cheek.'

"Hello, Elsie. What do I do?"

"Martinez is with me near the entrance. Where's your bodyguard?"

Al motioned with his head. "The fellow over there with the yellow striped pullover. He's heavily armed."

Elsie returned and reported to Martinez, never looking at the guard. Martinez studied the two men from his chair. To his chagrin, the guard's eyes met his. Rodolfo looked away. A few minutes later their eyes met again. Then again.

"Elsie!" he whispered. "The bodyguard's looking at me."

"Well, of course," said Elsie. "I just went over and talked to the man he's supposed to be guarding. The man kisses me on the cheek, then I come back and sit beside you. Of course he's going to look at you even if I do talk out of the side of my mouth."

Martinez bit his lip. "Tell Wheeler to check out."

As she did Martinez chose a lane of his own and started to bowl. Al strode to the counter; behind him lumbered the bodyguard whose omnipresent gaze met Martinez's. Martinez motioned for Elsie.

"Tell him it's off!" His whisper was loud and nervous. "That ape keeps looking at me. I can't make contact. We'll have to try someone else–someone without a gun."

Elsie motioned that the meeting was off. Martinez slid out while Al paid his bill then walked to Elsie and took her by the arm. "Okay, tell me what happened." For twenty minutes they strolled the mall arm in arm like lovers. Elsie finished her story and they decided that Bob Whitesides should meet Martinez at her apartment that evening.

"'Your policeman friend probably thinks you're seeing me on the side," said Elsie. "Tell your wife to forgive me." She chuckled, then off she went to join Martinez.

* * *

The room was darkish, basically brown, with stucco walls, braided rug, and heavy upholstered furniture. Bob and Elsie sat together on her couch, casually dressed. Across the table from them sat Martinez. His velour sneakers and sporty zip jacket, designed to give a relaxed look, were not working. Even in the dim lamp light his sweat glistened.

"Did Elsie tell you I have something you may be interested in?"

Ceremoniously, Martinez handed over the red folder and Chet's college ring. Bob fingered the gold. Perhaps just hours before Chet's hand had warmed it.

Martinez opened. "'Well, won't you consider what the M-19 is saying? These people believe in themselves. They think you're a thorn in the national flesh."

Bob remained silent.

"You folks think of yourselves as benevolent conquerors but Chester's hosts see things more clearly. They don't take kindly to your paternalism with the Indians. You have no respect for the sovereign dignity of native peoples."

"We have no respect for thieves and kidnappers."

Martinez ignored the comment. "The people I'm in contact with feel they cannot tolerate your presence in the country. As far as they're concerned, this pacification, this . . . pillaging of indigenous populations, it has to stop."

"I hear you, Rodolfo."

"The Institute paves the way for land expansion by the upper class. My contacts think—"

"I hear you, Rodolfo," interrupted Bob. "We know where M-19 stands. We're not sure they understand us. Have you explained to them about our interest in Bible translation?"

Rodolfo made sweeping motions with his hand. "Yes, yes, that's not important."

"Do you folks understand that we want to benefit the Indians?" Bob was offering bait: would Martinez refer to Chet's captors as "we" instead of "they"?

"Yes, but what these men are interested in is having their demands met."

"Is it money you want?"

Martinez grew impatient. "I'll ask. But the truly important question here is: Can you accede to their demands?"

The trenches were dug. An hour passed. Bob proposed an inspection tour of Lomalinda by a blue-ribbon panel—a group of respected Colombians of unquestioned patriotism from all walks of life.

Martinez would ask. A tour was not the point. "Why doesn't SIL have a Colombian to head its organization here?"

"You worked with us, Rodolfo. You know the answer to that. The organization works from the bottom up, not the top down. Everyone has a vote in who becomes director. One person's got as much chance as the next."

Empty coffee cups. Refilled. Emptied again.

Two hours.

Martinez's eyes twitched and his tongue played with his cheek. His nervousness permeated the room.

"These men are serious, Robert. They'll do as they've threatened. You really should listen to them."

"Why do I get the feeling you're less than neutral in this whole affair, Rodolfo? Your credibility leaves something to be desired."

Martinez nursed the comment.

"I want to ask something." The SIL man was pressing. He leaned forward. "Whom do you fear the most in all this? God or man?"

Martinez shifted.

"You haven't answered."

Slowly, with pained face, "For me, God is an idea, a concept—something you can't grab hold of. Man you can touch." His thumb and index finger rubbed and he added quietly, "The police you can touch."

Three hours. Stalemate.

They agreed to meet again the following night. At Bob's suggestion each of the three led in a short prayer for Chet. The atmosphere was awkward. Standing to leave, Martinez pocketed the ring he had earlier handed Bob and slid the documents under his arm. Bob shot a questioning look.

"You said my credibility was bad." said Martinez. "SIL's isn't so hot either." He reached for the door and hesitated. "There's still some good in me, Elsie."

The door shut.

Over the next two days Bob met twice with

Martinez, once at Elsie's, once at Wimpy's Hamburgers. Each encounter accomplished less. According to Martinez, M-19 wanted nothing of a visit to Lomalinda by respected Colombians—the guerrillas had all the information they needed. Worse still was SIL's inability to trust its gift-horse negotiator. Information shared in private discussion somehow found its way to the press. The morning after the Sunday-night meeting at Elsie's, a picture of Chet's ring appeared in *El Bogotano*, a paper widely believed to pay cash for exclusive interviews. Did Martinez have a money motive? Could a man who had once called for SIL's ouster from the country and showed no signs of change be relied upon? The questions flowed.

Days earlier, and independently of Martinez, friends of the Institute had put it in touch with a well-to-do Colombian businessman who pursued an unusual hobby. The high-level sales manager—code name "Raul" for anonymity's sake—moonlighted as a mediator in hostage situations. Acquaintances described him as "shrewd, tenacious, yet charming," a "superlative negotiator." He enjoyed the universal respect of his peers and, in true humanitarian spirit, worked for free. Bob, Will, and Al were interested but skeptical. Could even such a man help an organization that, on principle, could concede nothing that encouraged terrorism? Will met with Raul.

"In almost any hostage situation, money can force a solution," the man assured Will.

"But we're not prepared to offer money."

"What about to the Indians? What about blankets and food to the Indians? It would put your guerrilla friends in a favorable light—endow them with an air of humanitarianism—and give them a way to save face while in reality backing down. *And this is the key: giving them an out in which they don't lose face."*

The argument made sense. Raul was in.

For several days SIL followed a strategy of "let not thy left hand know what thy right hand doeth." As Martinez continued his talks with M-19, turning up nothing, Raul probed his contacts for an avenue of communication with the guerrillas—turning up nothing. SIL was in a box. Raul had the credentials, Martinez, the contacts.

On Tuesday, February 17, Bob met with Martinez to inform him of the new facts of life. He would no longer work alone; he would answer to a gentleman named Raul, to be met the following afternoon in the Tequendama Hotel lobby. Descriptions were given, passwords devised. Martinez swallowed—he no longer held all the cards. The ace had been trumped.

On Wednesday, one day before the terrorist deadline, the biggest news since the abduction of Chet splashed tabloid front pages. BITTERMAN'S CAPTORS "PROMISE" HIS LIFE AS DEADLINE NEARS—CAPTORS' CONDITION: PUBLISH MANIFESTO. Chet's hometown paper carried the story.

> The kidnappers of Lancaster missionary Chester A. Bitterman III promised Wednesday to let him live if newspapers in Colombia published a 21-page manifesto. . . . The guerrillas' offer, first reported in the Colombian press Wednesday, was confirmed by the U.S. State Department and the Colombian government only 24 hours before the deadline.

"I've been informed that the kidnappers now want, as sole condition for not killing Mr. Bitterman, the publication of a manifesto in the press," said Colombian Interior Minister German Zea Hernandez.

"Since in Colombia we have absolute freedom of the press, the newspapers are free to publish the kidnappers' manifesto or not," the Minister told the Associated Press. . . .

However, the leading daily newspaper, *El Tiempo*, said immediately it would not comply with the bargain. . . .

In Washington, D.C., a State Department official cautioned there was no mention by guerrillas of releasing Bitterman.

"They say if the document is published they will postpone the deadline. They do not say for how long," reported Elizabeth Cummings of the Department's Office of Combating Terrorism. . . .

According to a press spokesman at the U. S. Embassy there, the newspaper described the manifesto as "an extensive analysis of the political, economic and social situation of the country. . . ."

Bitterman's wife and two daughters, Anna Ruth, 3 and Esther Elisabeth, 1 1/2, are still in Bogota at the house where he was taken hostage by 7 hooded and heavily armed guerrillas a month ago. . . .

Chet's family and colleagues held their breath as they studied the papers. On the pages before them, in black and white, the guerrillas were sending signals. "We don't want to kill Chet," said the signals—for those with eyes to see. "We want a way out." Bob shot a knowing look at Will. Clearly, Martinez and Raul were walking toward an open door.

Thursday approached with ninth-inning frenzy. Headlines debated the likelihood of a 6:00 P.M. execution. American newspapers phoned the guest house in search of latest scoops. Calls, telegrams, and letters of support poured into Wycliffe headquarters from around the world. Six guerrillas raided a law school auditorium at the National University in Bogota, denouncing Jaime Bateman as a "traitor to the Colombian working class."

One, two, three, the details came rapid-fire. Eighty, ninety, a hundred, the coming night and day would leave it all in the dust.

On the Eve of the Nineteenth

"Okay, then it's Al on the draft, Bob will look it over, and you'll call me before going to print." Will's voice, soft but crisp, never lacked authority'. "You will call?"

Their expressions said yes. Al and Bob strode from the office.

The Institute's final communique would air tonight, February 18, an eleventh-hour scramble to squeeze the terrorists in the vice of public opinion. Al would work up the rough copy with Colombian friends of SIL, Bob would proof it in the afternoon, Will would give the final okay.

By the time Bob wrestled free of his desk and telephone the sun was dropping. He scurried to meet Al at a coffee shop and scanned the document. It looked good. Al was especially pleased with an inspired sentence proposing that Lomalinda be turned over to Indian leaders—rather than to the government—when SIL finished its work in Colombia some fifteen years hence.

Bob was pleased, too. So were the Colombian friends. Racing in Al's Chevy to the downtown office where they would make copies for media distribution, the men debated: Should they take the time to call Will and read the script? The 6:30 P.M. news deadline breathed heavily upon them. Missing it could sabotage the whole project. No, the document was fine. Will would approve.

An hour later they would very much wish they had called.

* * *

Seven chimes rang from the snow-covered steeple's of Lancaster, Pennsylvania, linking that historic brick town with the city of Bogota by common time zone. As the strains fell, members of Calvary Independent Church gathered for the midweek service. Having spent the day fasting and praying in their homes and at their jobs, they would now pray together. The usual order of service was abandoned. Pastor Eric Crichton stood at the front of the vaulted sanctuary and announced what all of them knew. The deadline for Chet was tomorrow. They needed to go to God.

"I believe God does act through prayer," the pastor said, reading a passage from the New Testament in which an angel from God released the apostle Peter from prison. He then solicited prayers for Chet and his family.

A hand went up from the congregation. Rev. Crichton acknowledged a man in his twenties, seated beside his family. "I think we should pray for the guerrillas, too," the man urged. "They need the Lord as much as anybody. . . ." Heads nodded in agreement with Curt Bitterman's request.

Then, in the words of a visiting Lancaster reporter, "two-by-two the worshipers got down on their knees, elbows on the red-cushioned pews, and prayed. They prayed for a half-hour, each in his own words, and the babble of 200 voices filled the church to the roof."

Mary Bitterman could not attend the meeting. Sitting at home with her elderly mother (the one to whom Chet had given water from the toilet years before), she held her own prayer vigil. Fifteen minutes into the hour the phone rang. A foreign tongue, barely audible over the static, greeted her. With difficulty she made out the syllables Mare-ee-bee-tare-mon.

"'Yes," she answered, "this is Mary Bitterman."

The overseas operator switched to the caller. "O's" and trilled "'r's" punctuated the static.

"'I cannot hear you," Mary said loudly.

The male voice did not alter.

"'This is Mary Bitterman."

"Aló?" came the male voice. "'Hablo con la Señora Mare-ee-bee-tare-mon, no?"

Mary clutched the receiver in frustration. "'I cannot understand you. No comprehend Spanish."

Finally, a second male voice offering labored, accented English came on.

"Good eve-en-ing, Mee-ziz Bee-tare-mon. We want to know what do you think about, eh, your son—the problems of your son here in Colombia?"

"And whom am I speaking to?"

"This is Radio Todelar from Bogota, Colombia."

"Radio what?"

"T-o-d-e-l-a-r. It's a great broadcasting system — radio system. We want to know what do you think about the problem that has your son here in Colombia?"

"'Well. . . ." Her mind raced. Was the interview live? How do I answer that? "Of course we would like to have him released."

Her words were translated for the original caller who repeated their Spanish equivalent in a sonorous voice. An announcer, thought Mary. She was live.

"Do you think that this Institute, eh, Summer Linguistic Institute here in Colombia, do you think is necessary to go out from this country? What do you think about this?"

"I am sorry. I cannot hear you."

Translation and elaboration for the public. This continued throughout the conversation.

"Would you like to listen to your son's voice from here, from Bogota?"

"Well . . . . sure."

"Okay, in a few minutes we're going to let you hear the voice. Would you like to make a call to the people that has your son?"

Pause. "You're, you're asking me if I want to talk, uh, send a message to them? Is that what you're saying?"

The translator and announcer conferred.

"No, she's not here in the radio station."

Huh? She who?

"But she has a message for you."

What are you talking about? This was getting ridiculous. *Where'd you—?*

"Would you like to make a call to the people that has your son?"

Mary smiled, wondering how United Nations conferences ever managed. "Well," she responded, "we would like them to release him, yes . . . . we really do not understand how their, uh, holding Chester will accomplish any purpose."

"'What are you thinking about your son in the last days?"

"I am thinking that he is in God's hands."

The caller played Chet's Spanish tape that had

aired in Bogota three days before. Asked if she understood Spanish, Mary replied that she knew only three or four words. The caller translated.

"I want to know what do you think, Mrs. Mary, about the voice of your son? When you listen, what do you feel?"

"I think it sounds like him," she replied. "The thoughts are going through my mind that we would just like these people to be gracious enough to let him go back to his family, who desire to have him very much. Uh, I don't quite comprehend what they would accomplish by taking his life. I do not think that that is going to change things there."

"Would you like to send any kind of words to the people that has your son?"

"Uh, I guess I would like to tell them . . . that we care about them as people. And, uh, we do not like to see this kind of differences among people."

"Have you been praying in your family today?"

Mary spoke deliberately. "Yes, very much. And more than just today."

Seconds later a technical difficulty abruptly choked off conversation.

* * *

"Yes, very much. And more than just today."

From the battery-powered radio on the stone mantle came Mary's voice, permeating the room. Brenda steadied her nerves on her mother-in-law's composure. Such dignity! The candles themselves seemed to hear and approve.

With her parents and daughters, Brenda sat on a living room couch opposite the cold fireplace, the barred picture window to her left overlooking the night. Tiny flames flickered in windows up and down the street. Evening blackout—she was glad the Gottfried's had invited them. Good friends.

The two families began to chat. Dinner and Mary's interview ("Funny at places, wasn't it?") had put them in a good mood. The conversation lightened. There was even some laughter.

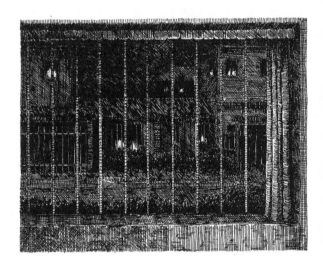

The radio programming continued. Soon came another news item: a new public statement had been issued by the Summer Linguistics Institute. Brenda caught the phrases: . . . under agreement signed with the Minister . . . scientific investigation of language and tongues . . . socioeconomic support . . . in approximately fifteen years . . . maintain intact the tongues and cultures. . . a large percentage of which are indigenous . . . . Everyone nodded. Al, Bob, and Will were certainly out beating the bushes.

Normal programming resumed, ignored by all. Coffee was served, sweetened with laughter. The shadows relaxed, cozy and no longer threatening. Discussion turned to Mary. To memories of Chet. To swapped stories of—

She heard the words but she did not hear them. They were too unbelievable. Over the past few days SIL and the terrorists had edged away from the brink of that unthinkable nightmare; signals had been sent and understood; media strategies carefully constructed. Exchanges had been delicate; wording was everything.

And now? Now the announcer was broadcasting a special bulletin. Someone had called the station— a man—claiming to represent Chet's captors. Fury, said the announcer, had been in his voice. The public declaration of SIL that it would remain fifteen more years in the country was the final straw. By reading the document, the station had "just signed Chester Bitterman's death warrant."

Her ears went deaf, her throat, dry. Brenda felt but did not feel the hot tears on her cheek, the anger and fear in her brain, the heartbeat of her girls snuggled close. As in a trance, she led the little ones upstairs to bed, anxious to be alone. Anna tugged at her sleeve with a dozen questions.

"Sweetie," Brenda replied, "those bad men who have papa want to kill him."

Uncomprehension crossed the tiny face. "Jesus won't let them, will he?"

Mama's silence spoke clearly enough. When the

sobbing had died and the eyelids fell, Brenda tucked the girl in. Little Anna drifted off to sleep, her lips framing the words, "When 1 am afraid 1 will trust, Lord, in you."

George Gardner was not content to sleep. He telephoned Will upset. Will telephoned Bob, enraged. "We've really done it now!" he fumed. An hour later Will's residence bulged with visitors: Al offering explanations, Rodolfo Martinez offering a Bogota radio producer ("He'll know what to do"), the producer introducing a free-lance writer.

"I want to rescind that communique," Will clipped.

"You can't."

"Why not?"

The producer huffed. "You can't just get on the air and say, 'Ladies and gentlemen, forget what we said yesterday. We didn't mean it.'"

"Okay, then," frowned Will, "what do we do?"

The radio man stared back. "You draft a revision. You explain what you meant."

Will pointed to the Colombian writer. "Can this man produce?"

"He's very good."

On the spot, Will hired him.

Sleeves were rolled up, paper produced, coffee perked. Martinez excused himself to locate Raul and reattempt some coup of diplomacy. Later, Al retired. On into the night Will and the writer toiled, weighing innuendoes, scratching phrases. Dawn was hinting when Al returned for the finished document, its ink still wet. The writer slid into the front passenger's seat and the two sped off. Their destination: every radio station in Bogota.

Twenty minutes later Will heard the first announcement over the airwaves. "Fifteen more years" had mellowed to "in the not-too-distant-future." Will sighed, relieved and exhausted. The phrasing would score.

Bob, too, heard the broadcast. His stomach churned. To his thinking the revision contained language as offensive as the original: ". . . in each [ethnic language] the work requires from seventeen to twenty years." People would still put two and two together: the Institute intended to remain for some time. What would he say when he saw Will in the office?

No one said anything in the office. Al was quiet—still smarting from the mistake. Bob bit his tongue—why cry over spilt milk? Will bit his—why harp on a past offense? The tension, just below the surface, lasted until the phone call.

"Are you certain? Certain?"

A smile sprouted on Will's face that paled the sun. "Brothers," he beamed as he set down the phone, "our man Raul hasn't been snoring all night. Neither has Martinez."

Al and Bob turned their heads.

"They've gotten us a fifteen-day extension."

The ice was water, then mist, then gone. Three brothers grinned at each other till their eyes squinted.

"Bingo!" said Bob.

✳ ✳ ✳

Thursday; Feb. 19.–10:00 P.M.
    I will praise you with the harp
    for your faithfulness, O my God;

I will sing praise to you with the lyre,
O Holy One of Israel. ...
My tongue will tell of your righteous. acts
all day long,
for those who wanted to harm me
have been put to shame and confusion.

Psalm 71 :22, 24)

Brenda poured her joy into her diary. An extension for her dearest! Fifteen days, two glorious weeks, provided that SIL agreed to a media blackout. "Provided that." Just what did a "blackout" mean? No words at all? Nothing about the translation work? About Chet? It didn't matter. It didn't matter. He was safe, alive. The photo had proved it.

There was Chet, as big as life, in the papers. Grinning. Playing chess. His beard back, bushy and masculine. In front sat a guard wearing army fatigues and a hand grenade. On the floor (Oh, it was wonderful!), on the floor lay newspapers, scattered about. Monday newspapers with headlines clearly visible. Chet was alive as of Monday. No doubt at all. It sent goosebumps through her, made her know he was still alive, today.

Everyone had been so helpful. Lomalinda had fasted and prayed all day. Columbia Bible College had called hourly and prayed around the clock. F-2 had checkpoints all over the city. Even *El Bogotano* pitched in, printing half of that guerrilla manifesto with promise of the second half if M-19 assured Chet's safety.

Friends: she loved them. The headlines BITTERMAN "SPARED" FOR FIFTEEN DAYS surged in her veins.

✳ ✳ ✳

Friday, Feb. 20-9:45 P.M.

> Surely in vain have I kept my heart
>> pure;
>> in vain I washed my hands in inno-
>> cence.
> All day long I have been plagued;
>> I have been punished every
>> morning.

(Psalm 73:14)

Brenda poured her frustration into her diary. No extension for her dearest! He would die tomorrow. 4:00 P.M.? 6:00 P.M.? Midnight? Everyone said something different. How was she to know? Her jaws tightened; she felt she might vomit.

It started yesterday afternoon—only hours after news of the extension—when that call came to the Gottfrieds.

"Who?" Panic in his eyes, Virgil Gottfried had asked the caller to repeat himself. "She's not here," he lied. He slammed down the phone and dialed Bob Whitesides. "Martinez called here," sputtered the pilot. "The terrorists insist on a personal talk with Brenda. I have no idea how he traced her whereabouts."

"We'll handle it," said Bob. "Thanks for calling."

Bob met with Will and Al, and together they decided to arrange a phone conversation between Brenda and the guerrillas; Martinez would be given a phone number to pass on, but no address. Consequently at 7:30 P.M. Brenda had found herself in the private study of Jack Murr, an American

223

businessman whom Will knew casually. Murr's earnings afforded him bodyguards and sophisticated electronic security. The place, said Bob, was perfect.

Brenda was still afraid. She had heard that the nation's phone system was peppered with radicals of every sort. Insiders might trace the call, pinpoint the address, tip off M-19.

"Don't get panicky. Don't make deals," coached Bob. "Get them to repeat for the recorder." Brenda shook; the wires and equipment unnerved her. She surveyed the wood paneling, wall-to-wall bookshelves, recessed lighting. Comfortable setting; too many people. Bob, Al, Murr, his wife, the maid, the guards, an associate—did the whole world have to come?

"Play dumb," Bob continued. "You're confused. Can't understand. Send them to Raul. He's their man."

She blinked, trying to absorb it. Bob was right. Send them to Raul. No use in a negotiator who didn't negotiate.

"He's your representative, not SIL's. Stress it. Make them feel you're sending them straight to the top."

Sending them, she thought. Why am I sending anyone anywhere? Why did they call me? Bob theorized that the guerrillas had lost faith in Martinez as too unpredictable and self-serving. They'd grown wary of SIL after it had defeated them in the media (hence, the forced news blackout). And Raul had never been accepted as truly representing SIL. So now they were going to the top: for her.

Send them to Raul, Brenda reminded herself. He's the top. Send them to Raul.

She glanced at her watch. Quarter after eight; fifteen minutes late. When no one called by nine the group went home.

Mrs. Murr had been hurrying out the door for a hairdresser's appointment the next morning when the phone rang. A male voice: "Is Brenda there?"

She reacted quickly. Brenda was out, but would return by eleven.

Ten forty-five found the group huddled again in Jack's study. Brenda sat uncomfortably, trying to envision her caller. A gentleman? A jailbird?

A hundred and forty-one suspected M-19 members had gone on trial yesterday in Bogota. Lively sorts. Even though the government was considering amnesty for those not accused of violent crimes, things had gotten out of hand. "The torturers cannot judge political prisoners!" they chanted filing into the courtroom. One had risen to protest: M-19 had nothing to do with Chet—the charge was a government trick to divide the movement.

The phone rang, silencing her thoughts. Murr answered, passed it to Brenda. Traffic roared in the background. A phone booth.

"Habla Brenda?" The conversation would be in Spanish.

"Yes. " Her heart all but stopped.

"You know we were supposed to kill Chester yesterday but—"

"Please repeat. I can't hear you."

Louder, but still rapidly. "You know we should have killed Chester yesterday but we didn't. We gave him twenty-four hours. But we won't act today because of the labor strike. We want to show solidarity for the ADO march."

"Please I do not understand."

The caller, frustrated. "Worker's Self-Defense Group. We will not distract attention from their demonstration today. But tomorrow—"

"Is Chet all right? How is his gall-bladder?"

"Señora! He is fine. This is not the point! Chester will die at 6:00 P.M. tomorrow if SIL doesn't get off their seats and do something."

The blood drained from her. What about the fifteen days? "I don't think I heard you good," she panted.

"I think you did."

Think quickly. "Pardon? Hello?"

"My time is up. I'll call back." Click.

The three minutes between calls were no break at all.

"Señora. Have you been following me?"

"There's a fifteen-day extension."

Pause. "A . . . a what? Where did—? As I said before, Chester is dead tomorrow. "

Brenda, in a panic. "Please repeat. Please repeat."

He repeated. SIL needed to get serious or pay the consequences.

"But what about the extension? What about . . . You need to see Raul. He is my personal representative."

"Señora, I am speaking to you." Boisterous engines nearly drowned his voice.

"I am unclear," stammered the faint, determined woman. "Raul speaks for me, not for SIL. Your words are fast and difficult. Talk to Raul."

"Mrs. Bitterman. Tomorrow at six."

"Talk to Raul. Talk to Raul."

"Okay, okay." The voice faded. "Tomorrow at six. "

Imbroglio

Tomorrow came and, with it, imbroglio. No one called Raul, but anonymous voices poured into SIL, the radio stations, and newspaper offices. Anarchy seized the lines.

"He's a dead man by four this afternoon."

" . . . by six P.M."

"Midnight tonight."

"Sunday. "

In the past, M-19 had done business by mail certifying ransom demands with photos of its hostage holding up current news headlines. Until Friday's call to Brenda, Chet's captors had honored tradition, sometimes substituting a ring or I.D. for a photo. But once word spread that the terrorists had taken to the phones, every prankster in Bogota, it seemed, sought recreation by calling in a spurious deadline. Unable to verify or discredit any, Brenda prayed through them all.

Meanwhile, the Worker's Self-Defense Group paraded as planned through the downtown streets, drawing smaller crowds than expected. *El Bogotano* published Bible quotations from Chet's recent letter to Brenda. Chet had cited only the references; *El Bogotano* printed the texts in full, filling a two-page spread. No amount of money from Christians could have brought such welcome exposure. Captioning a photo of the missing linguist were the words, "Nothing can separate us from the love of God demonstrated to us in Christ Jesus."

In hope that a news blackout would yet salvage Thursday's fifteen-day extension, SIL ceased all public comment. Newspapers and radio stations followed suit, disgusted with the array of contradictory "hot tips." Like the father of the prodigal straining at the horizon, Brenda awaited news of Chet. She would wait for the next ten days.

Saturday night. Sunday. Monday. Like a faucet's reluctant dripping, time refused to be rushed. The silence about Chet was the kind that sets you to studying tiles on the floor and playing with droplets of tea in the bottom of your cup, focusing on things you don't really care about, just to pass the time.

To the rest of the world, nothing had happened. Jackhammers still pounded at construction sites, car doors slammed, people dropped their change at cash registers, the coins rolling till they spun dizzily and exhausted themselves on the floor. Brenda stared at the shoppers, expecting something to happen (she did not know what), waiting for something *real* to rip apart the scene and leap out at her. But the scene itself was real—the shoppers, the coins, the store—just as Chet's disappearance was real. Two worlds, equally real, never meeting or speaking to each other.

She clung to her Bible, which daily seemed to promise that Chet was not dead. She clung to her parents who loved, and protected her and spent time with the girls. She appreciated the visits of Rev. Abadia, her Colombian pastor—although she was usually so numb she scarcely heard a word ("Thank you for coming"). But she wished someone would just call and tell her Chet was free and coming home, or that he'd died of gall-bladder failure, or that they'd poisoned him and buried him in a trash pile somewhere . . . or simply that he was alive . . . or something . . . anything. But this waiting was draining the life from her.

She was leaning against the tree in the side yard on Tuesday watching the girls on the seesaw. The whitewashed stone wall stood guard, keeping strangers out, her in. Limiting. Restraining. The girls rose and fell, up and down, laughing in the half-hearted way of children who almost, but never quite, forget that something awful is in the air. She could as well have been watching her spirits over the past five weeks, soaring and plummeting. The sky was blue. Her mood was blue. She was sufficiently upset that she wondered in what tone of voice the questions might rush from her mouth if God were suddenly to stand before her.

Bitter. She was out-and-out bitter. She'd never thought of it that way but it came clearly to her now. "God, the guerrillas, the entire cast. God was omnipotent—that was obvious enough. The Almighty. He could have prevented a half-dozen mortals from making off with her husband. Why hadn't he?

Yes. Why not? She began wondering whom a person could fully trust in a situation like this. God himself had been her trust since earliest childhood. Was her confidence misplaced? She pondered the question at length. Many unpleasantries had come during the course of her life. That, she realized, proved nothing in itself. A physician's needle feels unpleasant to a baby, but the older child understands. Looking back on most of life's calamities she could see that they came from superior wisdom

229

and a hand of kind intent. "Most" of life's calamities. What about the others? She pondered this, too. Had not God delivered his Son over to a crucifying mob on her behalf? Didn't that entitle him to a little trust from her?

If this awful thing had happened, God certainly knew about it—no, certainly had known about it beforehand, and allowed it anyway. And the Scriptures assured her that his acts are never senseless or capricious.

A thought began soaking into her, not a new thought, but one that had somehow never penetrated her emotional barricade and shaped her thinking about this situation. The longer she stood against the tree, the more she began seeing her husband's captivity as his job, a sort of special assignment for a man with a definite set of qualifications. God had chosen Chet to speak to these anarchists—whatever else was in the plan—and her duty was wholeheartedly to support him in prayer.

Brenda would labor with her emotions long after that Tuesday morning. But the side-yard bout to accept her husband's kidnapping was, in the words of Churchill, not the end, nor even the beginning of the end, but perhaps the end of the beginning.

The victory was well-timed. That very afternoon, February 24, the first of the final assault commenced. Papers and radios began reporting eyewitness accounts of a body spotted floating face-down in the Fucha River, a concrete canal zigzagging through Bogota. The body's hands were tied and its head covered with a hood. Severe thunderstorms delayed investigation. When police arrived, they found nothing.

Had it been Chet?

Several days later another corpse was discovered in a Bogota park, its arms eaten off with acid. No less disturbing was a front-page photo sighted by George Gardner at a newsstand as he and Brenda strolled a shopping-center. He hurried his daughter along grateful she had not noticed the photo or its caption: "Police search for the body of Chester Bitterman."

In a stilted, thatch-roof hut above the coastal waters of Indonesia a half-dozen tribesmen kneel in prayer for a linguist whom they have never met, held captive in a country they will never see. He is their brother.

The same day as the "floating body," one of the women at Lomalinda suffered a motorcycle accident, sustaining head injuries that spread an already-virile sinus infection. Within hours she fell into a coma. The center's doctor ordered her flown to Bogota, pessimistic about her survival. Institute morale dropped further. Two days later, in what doctors considered a near-miraculous reversal, the woman recovered.

She woke just in time for the bombings.

The first explosion ripped through the garage door of a townhouse in South Bogota where several SIL members rented rooms. Evening blackout had darkened the streets. The blast knocked several occupants to the floor, but the shrapnel and flying glass missed them by inches. A mob of several hundred gathered in the park across the street, then marched on the house—chanting angry slogans and clawing at the entrances. One translator had the presence of mind to chain shut what remained intact of the door, saving the house from pillage. By the time police had dispersed the crowd two hours later, a second bomb had exploded at the former SIL guest house in another section of town.

That night a man in police uniform rang the guest-house bell. An Institute administrator started for the door when one of the ladies screamed, "Don't let him in!" This set off a shouting match between the administrator (who could not hear the caller's words through the door) and those who feared a repeat of thirty-five days before when another uniformed man had rung.

The bombs had shattered nerves as well as glass.

Pete Manier sat up in his Lomalinda bed, straining at the night sounds, fingering his machete. What would he do when M-19 stormed the center? (Attack was surely imminent.) He would wait by the door with chair in hand. He would thrash with his machete wildly in the dark.

A sweat droplet ran to his lip. He listened to his heart. He chuckled. Then he laughed: a chair against a rifle, a machete stopping grenades. The guffawing and bed-rocking woke Marcia. He explained; soon she was snickering. Her head on his shoulder, they prayed to the Night Watchman of the universe.

The next thing Pete saw was the rising sun.

Brenda had trouble falling asleep after the bombings. The slam of a car door outside at night would set her mind to racing. Will a pipe bomb smash through the window? Will Chet appear at the door, accompanied? Is his limp body being dumped on the sidewalk? She began setting out clothes every night for herself and the children in case of a sudden evacuation.

Phone calls continued to plague the guest house. They carried threats—or just silence. One night George answered the phone only to hear the word "Hola, hola" repeatedly.

The morning after the bombings a Colombian news agency telephoned with a surprise question. "What's this we hear about Chet's being released?" Brenda's brother called as well, having heard the news over United Press International in Chicago. Immediately Brenda packed. But late that evening her luggage still sat at the door.

Three days later, UPI speculated publicly that the coming week, Chet's seventh in captivity, would be pivotal: Chet would die or be released. That evening, the terrorists broke silence for the first time in ten days. The occasion was a phone-in press conference sponsored by Rodolfo Martinez at his private office in the west of town. Approximately two dozen reporters gathered to interview an M-19 representative as he called intermittently from public telephone booths—his voice amplified by a small speaker. The guerrilla, calling himself Chucho, began by reading a statement: M-19 had broken off communications with SIL as of February 21 (the day after the phone call to Brenda) due to the Institute's uncompromising stance; SIL's leaders were keeping their members in the country by lying to them; SIL had offered money but M-19 would not sell Colombia's national sovereignty for any sum;[1] a program of harassment and annihila-

---

[1] In actuality, the Institute was never comfortable with, nor did it authorize, the offering of money by its negotiators.

tion had begun the night of the bombings and would continue until SIL was out of the country.

The statement done, the reporters began their questions. Would the guerrillas hold Mr. Bitterman indefinitely? (No.) Were the caller and his group dissidents of M-19? (On the contrary, they were M-19.) Why, then, had the M-19 directorate denied part in the kidnapping? (Internal problems; brotherly disagreements.)[2]

The calls came in spurts over several hours. "Please excuse me," Chucho said at one point, "we are playing cat and mouse with our friends in green." He repeatedly accused SIL of fabricating a fifteen-day extension to keep its own members on a string and force M-19 into a public gesture of good will. One reporter pursued the comment.

"Then you have had no contact about a fifteen-day extension?"

"There is no negotiation," answered the guerrilla.

"The negotiation is that they leave or we'll make them leave."

That very week a freighter makes its way through the swells of the winter Caribbean en route to Colombia. Its cargo: ten thousand copies of the first New Testament translated by Wycliffe personnel in Colombia, the fruit of twenty years labor on the Paez Indian language.

---

[2]Rodolfo Martinez once boasted that he had leaked a nonexistent extension of the guerrilla deadline to the press to force M-19's hand. If true, this would explain the terrorist belief that SIL had lied to its members about a fifteen-day extension. On the other hand, guerrilla comments at a second press conference imply that one of the guerrillas did—without authorization from superiors—grant an extension to Martinez. SIL was never able to ascertain the facts.

The reporter objected that the Institute had made clear its determination not to pull out. Chucho understood, saying the Institute was bringing violence on itself; the bombings were a foretaste. The reporter continued.

"The violence you would take, then, would be to execute Bitterman?"

"No. It's not him as a person. Concentration had been on his person. The others have not been forgotten."

"In other words, you plan the kidnapping of other members of the Institute?"

Chucho's tone was casual. "We don't call them kidnappings. We call them operations."

For Brenda and the rest of Wycliffe, even such threats remained secondary to a concern for Chet. Was he still alive? Reason told them yes; a hushed execution would not serve the terrorists' publicity needs. Yet, one exchange raised doubts. Recalling the spate of anonymous calls ten days earlier, a reporter from *El Tiempo* pressed the caller for credentials. Could the media be sent current photos of Chet, verifiably dated?

"Ah, well," said Chucho, "the photos that we sent you the last time . . . perhaps . . . no, we can't send photos now. There are none now. We can't take any now."

"You can't take any photos?"

"No."

"Why could you take them before?" asked the reporter.

"Well, because before . . . let me explain this. Sometimes you newsmen are hardheaded." Chucho, instead of explaining, rephrased the terrorist threat. He was interrupted.

"You're saying that you can't photograph Bitterman," said *El Tiempo*. "You mean by this that Bitterman is already dead?"

"I will leave that for you to decide."

The newsman rebounded: if photos were unobtainable, could reporters be sent a dated, handwritten message from Chet? Chucho called this impossible.

"Then, Bitterman is not alive," poked the reporter.

"I can't give you an answer at this very moment because I don't know if he's dead or not. I'm only a conduit of information. I don't have the authorization, and they didn't tell me."

"You don't have the ability to give us any kind of proof of Bitterman's life?"

"No. Not now."

Mary Bitterman stands at her ironing board. She prays for her son. "God, please free . . ." "Please let . . ." The words will not come; they have never come since the first day. Her heart allows her only one prayer. She offered it yesterday. And last week. She offers it now. "God, whatever you wish. Whatever brings honor to you."

The minute the reporters adjourned, news began traveling by wire and telephone that Chet may have been killed. That night, shortly after midnight, a journalist phoned the guest house from Lancaster, Pennsylvania. "What's this we hear about Chet's being dead?" Brenda and her parents were shocked. Not having attended the press conference (no one from SIL had gone on advice of Colombian friends), they were unaware of what had been discussed.

Headlines the next day reflected the uncertainty:

BITTERMAN FATE STILL A MYSTERY

GUERRILLA HINTS BITTERMAN MAY HAVE BEEN EXECUTED

And above Chet's photo, on the front page of Wednesday's *New York Times*:

REPORTED SLAIN: CHESTER ALLEN BITTERMAN III

Brenda refused to believe. That God would leave her in suspense with her stamina ebbing daily seemed inconceivable. Chet's parents joined her skepticism, as did the Institute. Satan, the father of lies, specialized in psychological warfare; the families would postpone grieving until a more certain word. Still, the lack of photos, tapes, or handwritten messages since the sixteenth of February chipped at their confidence.

As the week progressed, focus intensified on the supposedly granted fifteen-day extension. Martinez had called with the good news on February 19– the morning of the original deadline. Depending on how one reckoned (Colombians frequently include both first and last days when determining time), the countdown would end Thursday, March 5, or Friday, March 6—with Thursday the leading candidate.

Wednesday brought several discouragements of its own. In the morning, a private, Colombian owned DC-3 lifting from the Bogota airport lost both engines to sabotage, requiring a forced landing. The plane was identical to, and rented space beside, the Institute's DC-3. No one could help but wonder if the wrong plane had been victimized. The same day, Rodolfo Martinez was taken into custody by CAES agents for questioning on the

Bitterman case. He was soon released, but the incident buried what dying faith the Institute had in its negotiator. That afternoon *El Bogotano* printed another photo of a police search for the body of Chet.

In the evening, Brenda chatted with Chet's parents over the phone. Fearful of wiretaps and overdosed on hostage conversation, she remained distant and vague. They talked of snow in Lancaster, of the scale business, of where Brenda and Chet might stay after things returned to normal. Mr. Bitterman joked that, with Easter approaching, the terrorists might consider giving up Chet for Lent. Brenda chuckled unconvincingly.

On Friday, March 6, two days later, she learned of another press conference scheduled for that evening, but by then she no longer cared. She no longer felt. She had prayed all she knew how. Avoiding people and newspapers, she clung to her Bible. It alone did not disappoint.

Bob Whitesides did not plan to attend the conference. Informed friends judged the meeting a trap—the security risks high, the chance of a verbal slip great. In his place, as an Institute observer, went Adelmo Ruiz, a young Colombian who oversaw the SIL office. Adelmo had been on vacation when Chet disappeared and was anxious to help now in any way. Bob would await his call at the Ministry building.

The phone rang at 7:00 P.M., unexpectedly early. Adelmo spoke in quick, nervous sentences. There was little time. A guerrilla named Genaro was calling, angry. Why hadn't Wheeler come? He insisted that a high-level SIL man appear immediately. Otherwise, Chet was dead. If he came, they would prove Chet alive.

Bob hung up and considered his options. Will was out of town, in flight en route from Lomalinda. Raul's phone rang and rang—he could be anywhere. He dialed CAES and explained. A plan was set. Four bodyguards met him on the street below and the car sped out.

Ten minutes later they pulled up to a two-story, colonial home—now an office—with arched windows and stucco siding. Inside the fence, they strode to the door, gave their names, and entered. The door slammed behind.

They found themselves in a rectangular hall, stark but elegant, a curved stairway rising before them to the second floor. The guards fanned out except for one who ascended the stairs with Bob. Footsteps shuffled in the hall above. Bob looked up. Flash! Photographers. He covered his face with a notebook and pressed through the questioners with their note pads. Catching a glimpse of Adelmo in the hall he grabbed his elbow; together with Bob's bodyguard they disappeared into a side office. The door shut.

"Okay, give me the scoop," he said to Adelmo. "What's happening?"

Adelmo summarized. The conference had gone on since suppertime, calls coming at irregular intervals, never for more than five minutes. Genaro was upset at the absence of Al Wheeler and other important invitees. "When he learned I was here," Adelmo explained, "he asked me questions. I told him I couldn't answer, that I was just an observer. He said he thought I would answer that way, that I and my family and other Colombians working for the Institute were traitors, and that a popular revolutionary council was trying us at that moment He demanded we renounce the Institute and, to atone for our shame . . . ," his voice quivered, "that we Colombians leave the country."

Bob met the handsome brown eyes. Adelmo grinned weakly. "I told him I'd like to meet him and share about the love of Jesus. "

Bob grinned back. "What did he say to that?"

"He said, 'Yeah, right,' and hung up." Adelmo shrugged, then described how reporters had pressed Genaro to prove that his group had Chet. "That really got him angry. He rattled off names of M-I9 commanders held in La Picota prison—names not everyone would know—and asked if the media expected two of Chet's rings, or two I.D's."

"Do you think he's legit?" asked Bob. Adelmo nodded.

From across the hall they could hear Martinez's voice, loud and rough, shouting something about his lawyer's being there, and about not being responsible for things. Adelmo continued.

"When the female reporter asked what avenues of negotiation were left, Genaro said, 'None.' He said, 'Bring me someone from the Institute within twenty minutes who can give me a date when SIL will pullout and I'll provide firm evidence that Chester–'"

"He said what?" Bob's face darkened.

"He said, 'Bring me someone from the Institute within twenty minutes who can spell out when SIL will leave and I'll prove Chet is alive."

"Did you tell me that before?"

"What?"

"About promising a pullout date?"

Adelmo, blank-faced, "I think so."

Bob appeared stunned. "We shouldn't even be

here." He clicked his jaws, stifled an urge to slam the table, and stared at Adelmo. "What do we do now?" They decided to follow the original plan laid out with CAES. Bob would present himself, ask for proof of Chet's life, and refuse to make deals by phone. Someone knocked on the door. Genaro had called again. They stood, breathed deeply, and walked across the hall.

The door stood open to a sparsely furnished room dominated by an old oak desk behind which stood Martinez, his lawyer, and one or two friends. About twenty media people stood and sat about the office-only a few chairs lined the walls. On the I desk rested a telephone, jury-rigged to a tape recorder that doubled as an amplifier. Most of the men wore coats and ties; a few had open shirts. Martinez's tie was loosened and his collar un-buttoned. A half-empty bottle sat within reach of him and his friends.

As Bob came in, Genaro's voice could be heard over the recorder, eulogizing Martinez for publicly blaming the Institute for any stall in negotiations. Martinez glanced up with bloodshot eyes and said too loudly, "Genaro, Robert is here and wants to speak for SIL."

"Tell him to make a concrete proposal," said the guerrilla.

Bob took the receiver, prepared not to do business—a long shot alternative in his chamber. "Look, in order not to harm Rodolfo Martinez's reputation, why don't you call our office?"

"No," said Genaro. "I won't call the office. It's managed directly by the CIA."

"Don't you think these lines are tapped?"

"Sure, that's why I'm careful."

"Then listen. Why don't we speak in another country—Panama, Guatemala, or Miami, or wherever you wish."

"No! I will not speak. I won't negotiate any of this nonsense. I want you to tell me what day SIL will leave and I'll give proof Chester is alive. You hear? If you have something to tell me about a new position of the Institute, do if, because I'm going to hang up."

The words stung. It was as feared. Until a few minutes ago, Bob and his colleagues had believed the terrorists anxious to deal, eager for a face-saving way to release Chet. Now, the truth was dawning all too quickly. Bob collected his thoughts.

"We're ready to talk." Then, remembering Martinez's charge that the Institute was responsible for stalemates, he added, "We understand, too, that the one who pulls the trigger is the one who kills." The sentence just came to him. Bob did not know how.

The guerrilla replied, "Look, it seems that . . . I won't discuss this. My position is clear. Let me speak to Rodolfo; you and I can't understand each other."

Martinez took the phone and began fawning over Genaro, projecting that he would take any risks, go to any lengths. Genaro hung up.

Several more calls came that evening Bob and Adelmo huddled after each. The leak in the dike widened after every exchange.

Martinez: SIL can't leave in twelve hours or twenty-four. Is there a possibility of another limit?

Genaro: How many hours?

Martinez: Thirty-six, forty-eight hours?

Genaro: Well, make a proposal.

Martinez: I'll let you speak to Robert . . .

Whitesides: There is a plan.

Genaro: Tell me.

Whitesides: You're stubborn in saying fifteen years is too long.

Genaro: No, one more year is too long! If fifteen years is too long, one year is also too long.

Whitesides: What about Raul? Why don't you talk with Raul?

Genaro: No. I will speak only with SIL. I won't speak with people about people.

Intermission. Strategy. Prayer.

Genaro: What proposal can you make?

Whitesides: That we should talk.

Genaro: No, we are talking. But make a proposal because I can't stay here all night. How much time do you need?

Whitesides: Let's talk in Panama or at greater length.

Genaro: No, I will not negotiate the sovereignty of my country, and much less at a desk or out of the country. Here—with the national news media.

Whitesides: Neither can I alone dismantle a whole system.

Genaro: No? Well, then, there's nothing to say. I'll close.

Whitesides: I'm ready to talk, but not like this in fifteen minutes.

Genaro: But we haven't been talking fifteen minutes. We've been here since five o'clock. Give me Martinez.

Somewhere near 10:30 Bob left. A breeze awaited him outside. He could not recall ever being so tired. He arrived home, dialed Will with what he knew, and went to bed. That evening he slept deeply, dreamlessly. "There'll be big news to report tomorrow" . . . he had not stayed to hear Genaro's parting promise. Somehow, he knew it anyway.

How It Ended

They shot him just before dawn—a single bullet to the chest. Police found his body in the bus where he died, in a parking lot in the south of town. He was clean and shaven, his face relaxed. A guerrilla banner wrapped his remains. There were no signs of torture.

The driver testified that five men had chartered the bus an hour after midnight to transport a soccer team to the airport. En route to pick up the players, one of the five produced a pistol. They ushered the driver to the rear, tied and blindfolded him. One terrorist took the wheel. For a long time they drove about the city.

The bus stopped, several passengers boarded, and travel resumed. Then the radio clicked on to full volume. Picking up the song, the guerrillas joined in at the top of their voices. A shot rang out, unmistakable even in the clamor. The music stopped. There was more riding, then the bus slowed to a crawl. Feet shuffled out. The engine died.

After hesitating a minute the driver fought with his ropes. He freed himself and started for the front. In the aisle before him, two feet protruded from beneath a white flag.

Brenda got word early in the morning. Major Morales had called from CAES to ask for Will;

George gave him the number, sensing something amiss. As he replaced the phone, someone knocked on the door. It was the neighborhood grocer. Had they heard the news?

Will came by and drove Brenda and her father to the morgue. An army of newsmen awaited them. George and Will shielded Brenda as she ran the gauntlet to the gates. Inside the compound, she and her father walked to the open garage where the corpse lay, and where two guards held handkerchiefs to their nostrils.

"Daddy . . . I can't go in there."

George entered alone. He spotted Chet—the wavy hair, the peaceful face—draped in a sheet to his chest. Removing the right sock he confirmed a foot scar from a college motorcycle accident. The coroner would later report that Chet died within minutes of the shooting, his pain probably lessened by the sedative found in his bloodstream. Perhaps he had felt no pain at all. It is possible the terrorists had killed Chet only reluctantly and wished him to suffer as little as possible. George left.

"Is it him?"

Her father nodded. "He looks good."

For an hour they talked and cried in a side room. Finally, the doctor arrived to pronounce Chet dead. Al and Will drew the press to the front gates by starting up their car engines. Brenda and George slipped unnoticed out the back into an unmarked American Embassy van.

Back in the guest house, translator Jack Keels read to Anna Ruth as she sat on his lap. Her chubby finger pointed to a picture in the Bible story book. "That man is Jesus," she said. "My daddy's with him now."

Late in the morning a Colombian radio station interviewed Chet's parents by telephone in Pennsylvania. The father spoke in a steady voice. "I don't know what God plans to do with the death of my son. I guess we'll just have to wait and find out. I'm sorry I won't see Chet again in this life, but I know I'll see him again in heaven. Chet had a great love for the Colombian people; he wanted to tell the Indians about God. Now, I'm hoping someone else will go in his place."

Mary Bitterman also spoke. "What do we say to the Colombian people? Just that we love them. This gives us no ill feelings toward Colombia or Colombians. God loves them. So do we. We're hoping the guerrillas come to know God."

The program reached a nationwide audience.

All morning the American Embassy worked feverishly to speed procedures for the release of Chet's body. By three in the afternoon, all was ready. The family, the casket, and both Embassy and Institute officials met at the airport. Waiting on the tarmac by the DC-9 were a half dozen press cars. As at the morgue, Al Wheeler, drew the newsmen from Brenda to himself. "Have pity on Brenda," he said. "Fire at me." The invitation was take-charge, but friendly. They fired.

"We understand that you were the original terrorist target, and that Chester Bitterman died in your place. How does this make you feel?"

Al ran a hand through his hair in characteristic fashion. "That's right," he said. "He died in my place and it moved me very much. But Chet's not the first person to have done this for me." He collected his thoughts. "Two thousand years ago, Jesus Christ did the same thing—voluntarily. His life for mine. Anyone accepting Christ's death as sufficient payment for his sins receives the gift of eternal life."

Eager microphones. Scribbling pens.

"Are you planning to leave Colombia?"

Al, surprised, "Leave? No. My roots are here. I've had three children born here. I've been here eighteen years; I'm a part of this land. I have many friends here. No, I want to stay as long as the Colombian people want us."

The casket was loaded, the engines kicked over, and the plane lifted into the Colombian expanse. Over the rippling muscles of the Andes, down to the vast savannah. And finally, Lomalinda—an oasis of hills amid gentler swells.

His coffin was slid into the rear of a van that began moving slowly down the winding dirt roads. The people plodded behind—Wycliffe families, Indians, Colombians with sun-wrinkled necks from nearby Port—past the saw-grass, past the broadleaf plants, to the grave site on the edge of the field. Under parted skies they held a simple service. They sang hymns in Spanish and English, without accompaniment. Scriptures were read, Chet's life rehearsed. Soldiers mingled among the civilian crowd. Translator Tom Branks, a friend of Chet's, stepped to the microphone. Standing straight, the husky man folded his hands behind him. He spoke slowly.

"Seems strange to me, as short a time as I have known Chet, to be the one here who has known him the longest. I met him in Dallas where we studied together. I got to know him fairly well, both in the classroom and out."

"Two things about Chet came to mind today as

we sat in chapel, waiting for the plane. The one—
and it's something you all recognize—was his
always wanting to know the answers, his constantly
asking what it's all about. I don't suppose he
knew, while captured, that millions of people
around the world were forced to come face to face
with the bravery and holy courage of this man. And
I suspect Chet may have been a little discouraged
this morning."

Tom was weeping.

It was just a dream, really, a foolish one, I suppose. But I pictured Chet . . . after he had heard those words, 'Well, done, thou good and faithful servant.' . . . I pictured him saying, 'Lord, I never got to finish.'"

The mourners pressed close, oblivious to the heat. Fathers held their children in front of them.

"Then I thought of Chet playing soccer. It was Chet's manner to play the right, forward wing. You remember. He had a definite style—you could always count on it. Whenever he got the ball he would drive as far and hard into the opposition's territory as possible. Then he'd kick the ball across the center for someone else to score.

"I think the Lord said to Chet today, in a way none of us can understand, 'Chet, you carried the ball far, deep into the enemy's territory. You talked to those men, shared the gospel with them. You made them see what they're doing, and made them understand what the translators are all about. I let you do it. I knew that's the way you were.'"

Tom's eyes drifted, unfocused.

"Then I got to feeling that Chet really did carry the ball as far into opposition ground as possible." He met the eyes of his audience. "And now he's kicked the ball to us."

The prayers and speeches over, they gently lowered Chet's casket. Then they took up shovels and covered it with dirt. Colombian dirt. In a grave beside an Indian.

Epilogue: The Unexpected Beginning

The goal of Chet Bitterman's life was to broadcast the good news about Jesus Christ—the message that God in human flesh had borne the judgment due His own creation. He wished to have a part in filling St. John's prophecy of all nations, and kindred, and people, and tongues bowing in homage before Christ.

He reached his goal. Frustrated in his attempt to translate the Bible into Carijona, he preached instead to his captors. And through his capture and death the Christian gospel was proclaimed and lived out before Colombia's millions. His parents' interview, aired hourly throughout the afternoon and evening, stirred the national soul.

The Summer Institute of Linguistics reaped the benefits. Having languished in fear and uncertainty for seven weeks, it now basked in the effusive support that flowed from President Turbay on down. The guerrillas had intended to oust the translators; instead, they entrenched them. Almost a decade of negative press gave way to supportive editorials. Al Wheeler's reference to Colombia as his home tapped deep springs of patriotic sentiment. For a week strangers embraced Al in the streets, tearful and smiling. I saw you on television," they would say. We're glad you stayed."

Chet's burial in Colombia at his own request (a

contingency decision made upon his entering Wycliffe) was noted with awe. One Colombian official confided to an Institute acquaintance, "It was when I learned where he was buried that I *knew* you weren't CIA." Not all the nation's questions about the Institute were settled, but the answers had won a hearing. As one translator put it, "You'd have to be numb not to realize that we're still in Colombia because of Chet."

Nor did Chet's death affect Colombia alone. In memorial services across the United States, people of various ages stepped forward to fill in the ranks where Chet had fallen. In the year to follow, applications for overseas service with Wycliffe Bible Translators doubled. This trend has continued.

Three days after Chet's death, at a roadside customs checkpoint in rural southwest Colombia, customs officials uncovered a massive arms cache in a tractor trailer winding inland from the coast. The windfall interception spurred the immediate deployment of thousands of national troops to the area.

When M-19 launched an attack on several provincial towns the next day, the military was ready. Government forces annihilated two of the three invading columns within a week, and captured the third soon thereafter. Topping the list of prisoners were two of the M-19's ruling three, including Rosenberg Pabon Pabon, the celebrated "Commander One" of the Dominican Embassy takeover a year earlier.

In their maximum-security prison cells, M-19 members were allowed no visitors except government officials and two Canadian Christians—a husband and wife—who for several years had ministered within Colombia's prison system. The couple's social activism won the guerrillas' respect and opened the door for their Christian message. In June of that year, the couple secured permission for the touring Sports Ambassadors basketball team to square off against the M-19 players. At halftime, the Dallas–based Christian athletes shared accounts of God's dealing in their lives to a respectful, attentive audience. Contact between M-19 and Christian believers has continued.

The success of the military's sweep in early 1981, capturing as it did two of the three top M-19 leaders (only Jaime Bateman remained at large), dealt M-19 a stunning blow. Yet guerrilla resistance has continued in Colombia like an underground fire, its eradication elusive. In any given month, insurgent activity bars some translators from entering their tribal areas. As danger ebbs and linguists return, they sometimes find their tribal homes demolished. But work continues, either through Indian speakers visiting Lomalinda, or translators contenting themselves with analyzing back data. Despite continued threats, they maintain the course charted by the executive committee on the week following Chet's death:

Resolved: To recommit ourselves to God and to the completion of the task He has given us in Colombia.

In April 1982, as a gesture of international good will, the churches and civic groups of Lancaster County, Pennsylvania, presented an ambulance to the Colombia State of Meta the state in which Lomalinda is situated. Traveling to Colombia for the presentation were Chester and Mary Bitterman, parents of the slain linguist in whose honor the vehicle was given. At the ceremony Mary explained, "The reason we're able to do this is because God has taken the hatred from our hearts."

The Bittermans were unable to realize their goal of meeting captured M-19 members, but they were received by President Turbay on a day when he had canceled all other appointments due to illness. The reception's warmth surpassed mere courtesy. Chet stepped around to the president's side of the desk and produced a family picture. Naming each child in turn he smiled, "I have eight children and they're all alive. One's in heaven and seven are on earth." The president embraced him.

Although numerous suspects were arrested in the months following young Chet's death, his abductors have never been identified with certainty. It is most widely believed that blame lies with an M-19 splinter group whose precise relationship with the central directorate remains unclear. As for the other players in the drama:

Beth Van Ormer (Chet's high-school sweetheart) is a Short Term Assistant with the Summer Institute of Linguistics, teaching Institute children in the Philippine Islands.

Tim Thompson (Chet's mischievous college classmate) went on to graduate from Calvin College and Dallas Theological Seminary. He is now a lecturer in Bible at Midwest Messianic Center in St. Louis, Missouri.

David Tosi (Chet's college roommate and fellow cafeteria worker) went on to become a pastor under the auspices of Village Missions Incorporated. He has served churches in four states.

*In the two years following Chet's death, Al Wheeler, while retaining his full-time government-relations position with SIL completed translation and editing of the Siona New Testament. Printed copies have been entrusted to a merchant friend for distribution since guerrilla activity in the Siona area frequently renders Al's physical presence impossible. Al is currently working on a Siona grammar, dictionary, and ethnology, and provides consultant help for other translators.

*Will Kindberg continues as an administrator with SIL in Colombia. In December 1983, the Kindbergs lost their twenty-three-year-old son in a motorcycle accident at Lomalinda.

*Bob Whitesides and his family live in Guatemala City, Guatemala, where Bob serves as director of the Central American branch of SIL.

*Jaime Bateman (founder and chief commander of M-19) is believed to have died in a 1982 plane crash in Panama.

*Carlos Toledo Plata, M-19 leader and former Colombian Parliament member, was released from prison through a government amnesty in 1982. Reestablishing a private dental practice, he devoted much of his time to championing social and political causes through legal means. In August 1984, on the eve of participating in the signing of a government-guerrilla peace accord, he was shot to death in the street.

*Rosenberg Pabon Pabon (leader of the Dominican Embassy takeover) was also released from prison through a government amnesty. He is currently being sought by the police and military for subsequent crimes.

Brenda, now remarried, serves with her husband with SIL in Papua New Guinea.

The Carijona Indians have yet to see a word of Scripture in their own language.